# One Month with A King

*31 Lessons from the life of King David*

ANGEL W. DUNCAN, PHD

Copyright © 2018 Angel Duncan
All rights reserved.

No part of this publication may be reproduced, stored in a retrieval system or transmitted in any way by any means, electronic, mechanical, photocopy, recording or otherwise without the prior permission of the author except as provided by USA and International copyright law.

ISBN: 978-1978258945

Scripture quotations marked (KJV) are taken from *The Holy Bible King James Version*. Cambridge, England: Cambridge UP, 1611. Print.

"Scripture quotations taken from the Amplified® Bible (AMP), Copyright © 2015 by The Lockman Foundation Used by permission. www.Lockman.org"

Scripture quotations marked (NKJV) from the New King James Version®. Copyright © 1982 by Thomas Nelson, Inc. Used by permission. All rights reserved

Scripture quotations marked (NLT) are taken from the Holy Bible, New Living Translation, copyright © 1996, 2004, 2007 by Tyndale House Foundation. Used by permission of Tyndale House Publishers, Inc., Carol Stream, Illinois 60188. All rights reserved.

Scripture quotations marked (ESV) are taken from the English Standard Version®. The ESV® Bible (The Holy Bible, English Standard Version®). ESV® Permanent Text Edition® (2016). Copyright © 2001 by Crossway, a publishing ministry of Good News Publishers.

Scripture quotations marked (NASB) taken from the NEW AMERICAN STANDARD BIBLE®, Copyright © 1960,1962,1963,1968,1971,1972,1973,1975,1977,1995 by The Lockman Foundation. Used by permission.

Scripture quotations marked (NIV) taken from THE HOLY BIBLE, NEW INTERNATIONAL VERSION®, NIV® Copyright © 1973, 1978, 1984, 2011 by Biblica, Inc.® Used by permission. All rights reserved worldwide.

## DEDICATION

To my mother Brenda, who courageously chose to give me life so that I could exchange my life for a life hidden in Christ. I love you mom!

To my beloved siblings, may this book encourage you in your pursuit of the promises of God all the days of your life. I love you!

*"Set your mind on things above, not on things on the earth. For you died, and your life is hidden with Christ in God."*
**– Colossians 3:2-3 (NKJV)**

# TABLE OF CONTENTS

FOREWORD ......................................... I
ACKNOWLEDGEMENTS .............................IV
FEW ARE CHOSEN ........................................ 1
    INTRODUCTION ........................................ 2
    GOD LOVES EVEN THE LEAST OF US...... 3
    YOUR GIFT WILL MAKE ROOM FOR YOU
    .........................................................................12
    YOUR HEART QUALIFIES YOU ................19
PRODUCE IN REST ........................................ 25
    INTRODUCTION ........................................ 26
    BLOOM WHERE YOU ARE PLANTED .... 27
    HIDDENNESS IS NOT HOPELESSNESS 40
    GOD KNOWS WHERE TO FIND YOU ...... 46
REJECT REJECTION ...................................... 55
    INTRODUCTION ........................................ 56
    REJECTED BY MAN, CHOSEN BY GOD.. 57
    EARTHLY FATHERS MAY FAIL, OUR
    HEAVENLY FATHER WON'T ................... 66
    SUCCESS ATTRACTS JEALOUSY .............. 72
    SPEARS WILL FLY, BE PREPARED TO
    DUCK.............................................................. 78
    CRY OUT, ABBA FATHER ........................... 83
BRACE FOR BATTLE ..................................... 87

INTRODUCTION ............................. 88
DON'T FLEE, ADVANCE TOWARD YOUR ENEMY ............................. 89
UNCOMMON VICTORIES REQUIRE UNCOMMON TRAINING .................. 96
GOD ALONE CAN CAST THE FIRST STONE ............................. 108
INVISIBLE ARMOR, INVINCIBLE GOD . 113
AVOID IMAGINATION EXAGGERATION ............................. 118

## AS FOR CHARACTER? …FLAWLESS .......... 125

INTRODUCTION ............................. 126
BE EXCELLENT IN WHAT IS GOOD ...... 127
BE INNOCENT OF EVIL ..................... 132
DON'T STAY HOME DURING TIMES OF WAR ............................. 141
RETREAT TO THE PROMISE, NOT YOUR PAST ............................. 145

## LEAD TO SERVE ............................. 149

INTRODUCTION ............................. 150
GOD IS IN THE SHEPHERDING BUSINESS ............................. 151
GOD WILL SEND YOU APPRENTICES – EMBRACE THEM ............................. 155
GOD WILL SEND YOU ALLIES – RECOGNIZE THEM ............................. 160
SOW A LEADER, REAP AN ARMY ........... 164

## REPENT RAPIDLY ......................................... 169

### INTRODUCTION ....................................... 170
### GOD KEEPS HIS CONVENANT EVEN WHEN WE DON'T ........................................ 171
### REPENT IMMEDIATELY .......................... 174
### REPENTANCE CLEARS THE SIN, BUT NOT ITS CONSEQUENCES ....................... 178

## WORSHIP WHOLEHEARTEDLY ................ 183

### INTRODUCTION ....................................... 184
### PRIVATE WORSHIP PRECEDES PUBLIC WORSHIP ..................................................... 185
### ONLY GIVE GOD COSTLY GIFTS ............ 188
### WORSHIP GOD IN THE WILDERNESS .. 192
### WORSHIP GOD IN THE PALACE ............ 196

## FINAL WORDS............................................... 202

## REFERENCES ............................................... 203

## ABOUT THE AUTHOR ................................ 206

## FOREWORD

- Even though the gifts and calling of God are without repentance (Romans 11:29), it is ultimately the hearts of people that distinguish them as the chosen few who qualify to be used by God.
- God is concerned about the process of making you into the image of His Son, Jesus Christ.
- He will not stop, until the perfect work He began in your life is fully completed.
- The spirit of rejection must be rejected!
- We are not orphans. We can cry out to Abba Father, despite rejection by people.
- Our Father, God, has adopted us and accepted us as His children.
- Fulfilling your calling will not come without a fight!
- We must brace for the battles by embracing God's uncommon training strategies.
- How can we maintain a character that is flawless? Through our submission to the indwelling Holy Spirit.
- In order to lead people, you must *see the best* in them and *desire the best* for them.
- In the kingdom of God, leadership is defined through servanthood.

The above quotes are but a few of the gold nuggets of truth, found in the virtual literary gold mine that is - **ONE**

**MONTH WITH A KING** - waiting to be extracted by the reader who wants more than another book to read, but, is, instead, searching for material that will serve as building blocks for a life that can withstand the tests of time: joy and sorrow; storm and calm; peace and war; rejection and acceptance; servanthood and leadership; obscurity and greatness. The author, Dr. Angel Duncan, must be highly commended, in that, in this, being her first book, she has written with such conviction and maturity.

In this book, Dr. Duncan defies the stereotypical thinking that surfaces, when such a title is presented – 'Oh! That's just another devotional.' The mindset of such readers is that of seeing a booklet, presenting thirty-one or so pages, each of which carries either a scriptural passage, an anecdote, a testimony or some other offering, designed to satisfy the readers need for a quick pick-me-upper at the beginning of the designated day of the month. Sadly, though, when that month is over, both the booklet and its contents, more often than not, recede into oblivion, only to be seen again, most likely during spring or Christmas cleaning.

**ONE MONTH WITH A KING** is not your traditional morning devotional. Instead, Dr. Duncan's concept, behind this book, seems to be that of a clarion call to the reader who is in search of something deeper and more invasive than the one-a-day quick fix 'tablet'. In the process, she offers page after page of a nutritious diet of fresh revelation on which the reader can feast for days on end.

Moreover, by building this discourse on the life of David - the king, the worshipper, the giant killer, the mentor, the reject, the sinner – Dr. Duncan renders her book as being all inclusive, appealing to readers, male and female, from all stations and conditions of life. Her approach is not condemnatory. Rather, drawing on both her God-given gift and professional training as a life coach, she skillfully uses episodes in the life of David to correct, instruct and encourage the reader, not only to avoid the pitfalls of David, but, more so, to adopt the twin tenets of his philosophy of life, as recorded in Psalms 119:11 & 105 KJV:

- *Thy word have I hid in mine heart, that I might not sin against thee.* Ps 119:11 (KJV)
- *Thy word is a lamp unto my feet, and a light unto my path.* Psalms 119:105 (KJV)

So, it's time to open the book, get your pen, pencil and highlighters and begin the journey. I pray that the Lord will open up both your mind and spirit to receive, digest and apply the truths that you will encounter to your daily walk. One thing you must promise me, though, is that, as you see your life being transformed, recommend this book to both your friends and enemies. In fact, take it a step further and give one as a gift for a special occasion, such as a birthday or anniversary.

Apostle Vivian Duncan<br>
Divine Destiny Worship Centre<br>
Diego Martin<br>
Trinidad W.I.

# ACKNOWLEDGEMENTS

Thank you to my husband, Donnell, the trailblazer who inspired me to follow his lead and write my "first" book. I appreciate all of your prayers, love, and editing.

Thank you to my father, Pastor David Vickers who provided words of encouragement, wisdom, and knowledge throughout my life.

Thank you to my father-in-law, Apostle Emanuel Vivian Duncan who prophesied that this would be my first book and wrote an amazing foreword.

Thank you to my mother-in-law, Apostle Jemma Duncan who gave me the opportunity to write devotionals which birthed my love for writing.

Thank you to my mentors Beth Scott and Bonnie Wozniak who provided prayer, feedback, and encouragement and cheered me on in my calling in Christ. Thank you both.

Thank you to my intercessory prayer team Ben, Evelyn, Elder Franciene, Jade, Jessica, Kerry, Melissa, Minister Lucilda, Rosalind, and Sandra for your faithfulness in prayer.

I love you all!

# PART I
# FEW ARE CHOSEN

# INTRODUCTION

*"For many are called, but few are chosen."* - **Matthew 22:14 (NLT)**

God calls many individuals to come and partner with Him throughout the earth. However, very few accept His invitation. I have often wondered why so few of us reach out and embrace the hand of the One who is Faithful and True (Rev. 19:11). In surveying my own life, I marvel that I have found it hard sometimes to take a step when God asks me to move forward.

Do you know what I have come to realize? Even though the gifts and calling of God are without repentance (Romans 11:29), it is ultimately the hearts of people that distinguish them as the chosen few who qualify to be used by God. King David was one of those people. As a result, in his lifetime, he did everything God called him to do.

*"For David, after he had served the purpose of God in his own generation, fell asleep, and was laid among his fathers and underwent decay;"* - **Acts 13:36 (NKJV)**

In Part I, you will learn the following three lessons from the life of King David and along the way, complete the corresponding activities in the companion, **"One Month with A King: *Interactive Study Journal*"**:

1. God loves even the least of us
2. Your gift will make room for you
3. Your heart qualifies you

## LESSON ONE

## GOD LOVES EVEN THE LEAST OF US

*"Then Jesse called Abinadab and had him pass before Samuel. But Samuel said, "The Lord has not chosen this one either." Next Jesse had Shammah pass by. And Samuel said, "The Lord has not chosen him either." Jesse had seven of his sons pass before Samuel. But Samuel said to Jesse, "The Lord has not chosen [any of] these." -* **1 Samuel 16:8-10 (AMP)**

Have you ever compared your physical appearance, abilities, education or socioeconomic status to someone else? Have you ever felt that your attributes and accomplishments were sub-par to others around you? Have you ever felt that you did not measure up to the standards or expectations of other people? Have you ever felt that you were unworthy to serve as a vessel for God to use for great things? You are not alone.

I know I have felt these emotions at different junctures in my life. I was born to an 18-year old unwed high school student. Despite pressure from her family to have an abortion, she courageously chose to allow me to live and named me "Angel." As a teen mother, she had many questions and difficulties as a parent, but she knew that abortion was not the answer.

For my mother, the years following my birth were filled with unimaginable hardship, deep heartache, family rejection, and profound loneliness. However, she recounts that she always found joy when she looked into her baby's eyes. She knew that God still had a plan for her "Angel".

As a child, I often felt ashamed because I did not have the same family life as many of my elementary school peers. I did not have nice clothes, toys, or memorable family gatherings during the holidays. At times, there was not enough food for the whole family to eat so mom went without. In fact, I vividly remember poverty, domestic violence and emotional turmoil all around me.

Because of this atmosphere, my heart was broken, and my grades suffered in the earliest years of my childhood. They enemy caused me to believe that I was undeserving of anything good nor could I aspire to anything greater than my childhood environment. I often told myself; *"You're not smart enough to do well in school"* or *"You don't have the right family background for success"*.

Those statements were disqualifying, self-defeating, and even prideful. They were excuses to justify my belief that God could not use me to complete a great calling. Twelve years later, my mother courageously fled that dysfunctional relationship and began a new life in another state.

Miraculously, my mother also arranged for me to reunite with my biological father who had become a born-again Christian. He and his church family spent years interceding for my protection and salvation. Thus, the day I accompanied him to church was a direct answer to prayer. For a whole year, I attended Tuesday night youth group and Sunday services with my father and my stepmother. However, my heart was still broken, and I felt confused and all alone.

I will never forget the Tuesday night that Brother John Benedict the guitarist from the worship team filled in for the youth pastor. At the end of his sermon, he gave the altar call for salvation. With all heads bowed and every eye closed, I distinctly remember him uttering *"If your heart is broken, Jesus can heal your broken heart."* As soon as I heard this invitation, I raised my hand.

At the age of 13, I accepted Jesus as my Lord and Savior. When I glanced back at my dad, I could see that he was weeping too. Then he came and stood with me at the altar. Through my tears, I looked up at my dad and said, *"I don't know why I can't stop crying."* He responded, *"It's ok, Jesus is touching your heart."* I wept at the altar for what seemed like two hours. From that moment, Jesus healed and restored the pieces of my broken heart just like He promised in Isaiah 61:1.

> *"The Spirit of the Lord God is upon Me, because the Lord has anointed Me to preach good tidings to the poor; He has sent Me to heal the brokenhearted, to proclaim liberty to the captives, and the opening of the prison to those who are bound;"* – **Isaiah 61:1(NKJV)**

That same year, my grades dramatically improved and I became valedictorian of my sixth-grade class. Over the years, I have seen the Lord perform many miracles in every area of my life.

I have learned from personal experience that your family history does not limit God. The choices that your parents may have made also do not limit God. It does not matter to God how inadequately gifted you feel you are. It does not even matter to God what people think or prefer. God is no respecter of persons (Acts 10:34). God's **favor** plus your **willing heart** equal **success**!

Equation: **(GF + WH) = S**

Even if you don't have a tertiary education, struggle with a physical impairment or were born into a dysfunctional family; God can and will still use you. So it's time to shift your focus away from your inabilities and toward God's infinite ability.

> *"Then Samuel said to Jesse, "Are all your sons here?" Jesse replied, "There is still one left, the youngest; he is tending the sheep." Samuel said to Jesse, "Send word and bring him; because we will not sit down [to eat the sacrificial meal] until he comes here. So Jesse sent word and brought him in. Now he had a ruddy complexion, with beautiful eyes and a handsome appearance. The LORD said [to Samuel], "Arise, anoint him; for this is he."* - **1 Samuel 16:11-12 (AMP)**

The scriptures tell us in 1 Samuel 16:11-12 that David was young and ruddy. While his brothers were big, strong, trained members of Saul's army, David was a shepherd. To the natural eye, he was the least likely of Jesse's offspring to be chosen and anointed by the Prophet Samuel to be king. Yet, the process of receiving the king's anointing was just the beginning for David.

As his journey to the throne continued, he was invited to serve in the palace and bring deliverance to the spiritually oppressed King Saul through anointed music. Then one day he met a "giant" opponent named Goliath.

> *"Then Saul said to David, "You are not able to go against this Philistine to fight him. For you are [only] a young man and he has been a warrior since his youth."* - **1 Samuel 17:33 (AMP)**

> *"When the Philistine looked and saw David, he disdained him; for he was but a youth, and ruddy, with a handsome appearance. The Philistine said to David, "Am I a dog, that you come to me with sticks?" And the Philistine cursed David by his gods. The Philistine also said to David, "Come to me, and I will give your flesh to the birds of the sky and the beasts of the field."* - **1 Samuel 17:42-44 (AMP)**

Even Goliath was taken aback by David's small stature mockingly calling him a "boy". This Philistine champion from Gath who had been terrorizing the Israelites couldn't believe David was willing to challenge him when everyone else could only run away. The name Goliath means **"to uncover, remove, or go into exile"** so just the mention of his name struck fear.

Ironically, David's hiddenness would soon be **uncovered** because his defeat of Goliath would catapult him to the world's stage (1 Sam. 17:46). All his adversaries would be **removed** by God who would grant him peace on every side (2 Sam. 7:1). Yet, after defeating Goliath, David still experienced seasons of **exile** while running from King Saul and his son Absalom (1 Sam. 24 & 2 Sam. 16).

> *"But the LORD said to Samuel, "Do not look at his appearance or at the height of his stature, because I have rejected him. For the LORD sees not as man sees; for man*

*looks at the outward appearance, but the LORD looks at the heart."* - **1 Samuel 16:7 (AMP)**

Though David was the least likely choice among many, his heart for God made him God's choice to be king. Human beings, on the other hand, tend to be attracted to outward appearances. As has been demonstrated through the popularity contests in our society, people select leaders based on image, charisma, eloquence, marketing and public relations instead of honesty, integrity and character.

That's why we need to think like God. He loves everyone equally and has demonstrated His great love for all mankind through His Son, Jesus. We know this because He tells us in John 3:16(NKJV); *"For God so loved the world that He gave His only begotten Son, that whoever believes in Him should not perish but have everlasting life."*

However, God especially enjoys demonstrating His unfathomable love to and through the vessels that the world considers the least. The Bible is replete with examples of God's great love for the least. He takes great pleasure in using those things that are considered foolish in this world to demonstrate His wisdom.

> *For you see your calling, brethren, that not many wise according to the flesh, not many mighty, not many noble, are called. But God has chosen the foolish things of the world to put to shame the wise, and God has chosen the weak things of the world to put to shame the things which are mighty; and the base things of the world and the things which are despised God has chosen, and the things which are not, to bring to nothing the things that are, that no flesh should glory in His presence. But of Him you are in Christ*

*Jesus, who became for us wisdom from God—and righteousness and sanctification and redemption— that, as it is written, "He who glories, let him glory in the Lord."*
- **1 Corinthians 1:26-31 (NKJV)**

All throughout the scriptures, we observe an interesting trend with starting with God's selection of the small nation of Israel as His chosen people.

*"The LORD did not love you and choose you because you were greater in number than any of the other peoples, for you were the fewest of all peoples."* - **Deuteronomy 7:7 (AMP)**

The trend continued with God calling ineloquent Moses to be His Voice to Pharaoh.

*"Then Moses said to the LORD, "Please, Lord, I am not a man of words (eloquent, fluent), neither before nor since You have spoken to Your servant; for I am slow of speech and tongue."* - **Exodus 4:10 (AMP)**

What is even more remarkable is how God chose Gideon to rescue Israel despite his family's reputation or his status.

*"But Gideon said to Him, "Please Lord, how am I to rescue Israel? Behold, my family is the least [significant] in Manasseh, and I am the youngest (smallest) in my father's house."* - **Judges 6:15 (AMP)**

Consider the mustard seed. It might look small but what it contains on the inside is huge.

> *"He gave them another parable [to consider], saying, 'The kingdom of heaven is like a mustard seed, which a man took and sowed in his field; and of all the seeds [planted in the region] it is the smallest, but when it has grown it is the largest of the garden herbs and becomes a tree, so that THE BIRDS OF THE AIR FIND SHELTER IN ITS BRANCHES."* - **Matthew 13:31-32 (AMP)**

Like a mustard seed, the potential of your gifts may seem small or even invisible to the natural eye. You may not even be aware of all the gifts that God has placed inside of you and feel ill-equipped for your calling. However, God knows the great potential hidden in you so submit your life to Him. Take note of the following from the parable; *"a man took and sowed... when it has grown, it is the largest of garden herbs and becomes a tree."*

To see the manifestation of the gifts that God placed within us, we must sow or submit them to God in an act of submission. Then when we sow our gifts to God, He will cause us to grow into our full potential and have the kind of impact only He could dream of.

There are so many examples in scripture that provide insight into God's character and humility is one trait He embodies and enjoys. We know this because of His decisions to utilize humble heroes like Abraham, Moses, Daniel, and Rahab. From the birth of our glorious Savior Jesus in a humble manger, to His gruesome death on a rugged cross, God demonstrates His proclivity for humility.

> *"Now in a large house there are not only vessels and objects of gold and silver, but also vessels and objects of wood and*

*of earthenware, and some are for honorable (noble, good) use and some for dishonorable (ignoble, common)."* - **2 Timothy 2:20 (AMP)**

*"To console those who mourn in Zion, to give them beauty for ashes, the oil of joy for mourning, the garment of praise for the spirit of heaviness; that they may be called trees of righteousness, the planting of the Lord, that He may be glorified."* - **Isaiah 61:3 (NKJV)**

Remember that despite your physical appearance, education or socioeconomic status, God **can** use you for His glory. His love for you is great and the wondrous works He can do through you are immeasurable. **Today, He has chosen you to be a vessel for greatness!**

❖ Now turn to Lesson One in your companion "**One Month with A King: Interactive Study Journal"** to complete the corresponding GEM.

## LESSON TWO

## YOUR GIFT WILL MAKE ROOM FOR YOU

> *"One of the servants said to Saul, "One of Jesse's sons from Bethlehem is a talented harp player. Not only that— he is a brave warrior, a man of war, and has good judgment. He is also a fine-looking young man, and the Lord is with him."* - **1 Samuel 16:18 (NLT)**

Our Heavenly Father loves to give. He has established Himself as the greatest giver of all time by giving us the gift of Salvation through His precious Son, Jesus Christ. We truly cannot out-give God. In like manner, when Jesus ascended, He freely distributed an array of gifts to all of mankind. Not one, nor a few, but enough gifts for every human being willing to receive them came from Jesus. This means that each one of us has gifts and have been ordained by God to fulfill His unique purpose for our lives.

> *"God saved you by his grace when you believed. And you can't take credit for this; it is a gift from God. Salvation is not a reward for the good things we have done, so none of us can boast about it. For we are God's masterpiece. He has created us anew in Christ Jesus, so we can do the good things he planned for us long ago."* - **Ephesians 2:8-10 (NLT)**

> *"When he ascended on high, he took many captives and gave gifts to his people."* - **Ephesians 4:8 (NIV)**

Reality is that no one else can fulfill the purpose God has for you except you. Your purpose is unique, and there is not another human being who can do a better job at being YOU, than you can! This truth should boost your confidence in God's wisdom and sovereignty in choosing the unique combination of your giftings. Psalms 139:13-14 reminds us that *"He knit us together in our mother's womb."* This means He wanted you, designed you and custom-made you just the way you are.

> *"For we are God's handiwork, created in Christ Jesus to do good works, which God prepared in advance for us to do."* – **Ephesians 2:10 (NIV)**

Find comfort in knowing that the gifts God has placed within you cannot be hidden or go unnoticed. Even if you currently feel underappreciated or underutilized at home, work, school, in your local community, or even church, trust God's plan. The season will change, and your gifts will not remain hidden forever.

> *"You are the light of the world. A city set on a hill cannot be hidden; nor does anyone light a lamp and put it under a basket, but on the lampstand, and it gives light to all who are in the house. Let your light shine before men in such a way that they may see your good works, and glorify your Father who is in heaven"* - **Matthew 5:14-16 (NASB)**

God is a good Father. There is no earthly father who cares for his children better than God. As a good Father, He only knows how to give His children good gifts (Matthew 7:11) so every gift that God has placed in you is good and was designed to give Him glory. Notably, every good gift comes from above (James 1: 17-18).

> *"Every good gift and every perfect gift is from above, and comes down from the Father of lights, with whom there is no variation or shadow of turning. Of His own will He brought us forth by the word of truth, that we might be a kind of first fruits of His creatures."* – **James 1:17-18**

**(NKJV)**

*"If you then, being evil, know how to give good gifts to your children, how much more will your Father who is in heaven give good things to those who ask Him!"* – **Matthew 7:11 (NKJV)**

God sees every gift that He has given you as good, beautiful, perfect, and glorious! When you submit these gifts to the Lordship of Jesus Christ, over time they will begin to flourish, function, and fulfill the purpose for which they were designed. Then when your gifts become evident **in due season**, they will make room for you (Prov. 18:16). This is God's promise concerning the gifts that He has tailor-made for our lives.

*"A man's gift makes room for him and brings him before great men."* - **Proverbs 18:16 (NKJV)**

*And let us not grow weary while doing good, for in due season we shall reap if we do not lose heart.* - **Galatians 6:9 (NKJV)**

Unlike God, the enemy despises these gifts and desires to manipulate, abuse, suppress, and pervert them. One of his greatest tactics is to cause us to grow impatient with the process. Unfortunately, countless gifted individuals have been lured into the enemy's snare because they couldn't wait on God. In their haste, they prematurely "jumped" out of the hands of God before their season and failed to realize their full potential.

*"Saul's servants said to him, "Behold, an evil spirit from God is tormenting you. Let our lord now command your servants who are here before you to find a man who plays skillfully on the harp; and when the evil spirit from God is on you, he shall play the harp with his hand, and you*

> *will be well." So Saul told his servants, "Find me a man who plays well and bring him to me." One of the young men said, "Behold, I have seen a son of Jesse the Bethlehemite who is a **skillful musician, a brave and competent man, a warrior, discerning (prudent, eloquent) in speech, and a handsome man; and the LORD is with him."** So Saul sent messengers to Jesse and said, "Send me David your son, who is with the flock."* - **1 Samuel 16:15-19 (AMP) (emphasis mine)**

Though David was hidden in the wilderness tending sheep, his gift did not go unnoticed. Saul's servant, unbeknownst to David, was observing him. At the right time the servant recommended David to Saul based on his talent, character, appearance, and faith.

Through careful observation, we can see that there was a precise time, place, and people destined to be impacted by David's life. You see, David's gift of music could not remain hidden from the world. **In due season**, his gift made room for him to play before King Saul in the palace. David's life changed from that moment forward and The Lord remained with him on the entire journey.

What started as an invitation to play music in King Saul's palace ended with David becoming the best King in Israel's history. Like David, your gifts are for a designated **time, place,** and **people**. It was God who opened the door of ministry for David to utilize his gift. However, with that open door of opportunity, came dangerous opposition to David's obedience.

> *"Now it came about on the next day that an evil spirit from God came forcefully on Saul, and he raved [madly] inside his house, while David was playing the harp with his hand, as usual; and there was a spear in Saul's hand.*

# ONE MONTH WITH A KING

*[Handwritten margin note: Isn't it crazy that David was the one having spears thrown at him, but it was Saul who was afraid? Why? Because the Lord was with David.]*

*Saul hurled the spear, for he thought, "I will pin David to the wall." But David evaded him twice. <u>Now Saul was afraid of David, because the LORD was with him, but</u> had departed from Saul. So Saul had David removed from his presence and appointed him as his commander of a thousand; and he publicly associated with the people. David acted wisely and prospered in all his ways, and the <u>LORD was with him</u>. When Saul saw that he was prospering greatly, he was afraid of him. But all Israel and Judah loved David, because he publicly associated with them."* - **1 Samuel 18:10-16 (AMP)**

One valuable lesson I learned from Apostle Ann Marie Alman, pastor of People of Destiny Ministries International is to "<u>*give ministry positions to those who are already doing the work*</u>!"

*In his grace, God has given us different gifts for doing certain things well. So if God has given you the ability to prophesy, speak out with as much faith as God has given you. If your gift is serving others, serve them well. If you are a teacher, teach well. If your gift is to encourage others, be encouraging. If it is giving, give generously. If God has given you leadership ability, take the responsibility seriously. And if you have a gift for showing kindness to others, do it gladly.* - **Romans 12:6-8 (NLT)**

If you are called to be in the dance ministry, you will probably dance naturally during worship. If you are called to be an evangelist, you will naturally witness and bring many converts to the church. If you are called to hospitality, you will naturally serve others.

While you wait for God to open that big door of your dreams use your gifts to serve others right where you are. Continue to pray, submit, and listen to the voice of the Holy Spirit. God will speak to your leaders and at the right time, you will be given the formal opportunity to minister with your gift. You must pre-determine to obediently use your gift even when faced with fear or opposition.

I love the following story about Elisabeth Elliot from Everyday Answers with Joyce Meyer (joycemeyer.org);

> *"Elisabeth Elliot, whose husband was killed along with four other missionaries in Ecuador, says that her life was completely controlled by fear. Every time she started to step out to minister, fear stopped her. Then a friend told her something that set her free. Her friend said,* **"Why don't you do it afraid?"** *Elisabeth listened and took that advice. Together with Rachel Saint, the sister of one of the murdered missionaries, they went on to evangelize the Indian tribes of Ecuador, including the very people who had killed their loved ones. Many times, we think we should wait to do something until we are no longer afraid. But if we did, we'd probably accomplish very little for God, for others, or even for ourselves."* – ***Do It Afraid*** **by Joyce Meyer**

What would have happened if Elisabeth Elliot chose to allow the enemy to intimidate her? How long would she have waited for the fear to leave before doing God's Will? No one could have prevented Elisabeth from fulfilling her calling, except her.

What would have happened if David allowed fear to cause him to reject King Saul's invitation to play music in the palace? What if David allowed fear to prevent him from fighting Goliath?

What would happen to you if you allow fear to stop you from using your gifts? What would happen if you allowed impatience to cause you to step out of God's divine process? No one can prevent you from fulfilling the destiny that God has for your life, except you. Not even the devil can force you to stop. It's your choice! You are the only one who has the power to limit or halt your progress entirely.

Learn from David's example and not allow fear to prevent you from using your gifts when God opens a door of opportunity. Remember, your gift will make room for you but only **in due season**. Thus, despite how you feel, step out in faith and let your light shine!

- ❖ Now turn to Lesson Two in your companion **"One Month with A King: *Interactive Study Journal"*** to complete the corresponding GEM.

## LESSON THREE

## YOUR HEART QUALIFIES YOU

> *"After removing Saul, he made David their king. God testified concerning him: 'I have found David son of Jesse, a man after my own heart; he will do everything I want him to do."* – **Acts 13:22 (NIV)**

God is looking for hearts that are loyal to Him (2 Chr. 16:9). What keeps so many of us from having loyal hearts? One word; distractions. The sole purpose of distractions is to cause us to lower the guard around our hearts and shift the focus of our hearts away from the priorities of God. It's then easy to mistake human priorities for God's priorities, resulting in disloyal hearts.

> *"For the eyes of the LORD move to and fro throughout the earth so that He may support those whose heart is completely His. You have acted foolishly in this; therefore, from now on you will have wars."* - **2 Chronicles 16:9 (AMP)**

God is looking for people whose hearts are completely devoted to Him. How do you cultivate a heart that is devoted to Him? One word; **intimacy**. God desires that we spend time intentionally knowing and growing in our relationship with Him. As the church, we are the bride of Christ. In an earthly marriage relationship, intimacy plays a vital role in knitting the hearts of a couple together. Also, in a marriage, good spouses tend to learn each other's priorities.

Do you know what God's priorities are? They are clearly shown in the life of Jesus. God's heart beats for intimate fellowship with His children (Matthew 1:35), reaching lost souls (Matthew 9:35-38), restoring broken lives (Matthew 10:8), worshiping in spirit and truth without hypocrisy (Matthew 23:13 & John 4:24), love (Luke 10:25-29), serving others (John 13:3-5), and equipping leaders (Matthew 10:1). This is just a sample, but you get the point.

When we shift our focus away from God's priorities, our hearts are steadily drawn away from doing God's Will like a boat on a lake that is unanchored. Despite how close it is to shore or how calm the water looks, when unanchored, the vessel will drift far way over time.

> *"For all that is in the world—the lust and sensual craving of the flesh and the lust and longing of the eyes and the boastful pride of life [pretentious confidence in one's resources or in the stability of earthly things]—these do not come from the Father, but are from the world."* – **1 John 2:16 (AMP)**

> *"Therefore rejoice, O heavens and you who dwell in them [in the presence of God]. Woe to the earth and the sea, because the devil has come down to you in great wrath, knowing that he has only a short time [remaining]!"* – **Revelation 12:12 (AMP)**

In the world, everything is geared toward appeasing the lust of the eyes, lust of the flesh, and the pride of life. As the enemy's time draws closer to an end, he is feverishly intensifying the levels of these distractions. Despite this escalation, God is still actively searching for those whose hearts are after His heart and remain committed to His priorities through intimacy.

> *"Guard your heart above all else, for it determines the course of your life."* – **Proverbs 4:23 (NLT)**

# ONE MONTH WITH A KING

*"Your word I have treasured and stored in my heart, that I may not sin against You."* – **Psalm 119:11 (AMP)**

Your heart is where all your decisions concerning life are made. Your heart must be guarded and filled with the Word of God so that you will not sin against God. It is the condition of your heart that qualifies you to be chosen by God for greatness.

> *"Samuel said to Saul, "You have acted foolishly; you have not kept the commandment of the LORD your God, which He commanded you, for [if you had obeyed] the LORD would have established your kingdom over Israel forever. But now your kingdom shall not endure. The LORD has sought out for Himself a man (David) after His own heart, and the LORD has appointed him as leader and ruler over His people, because you have not kept (obeyed) what the LORD commanded you."* – **1 Samuel 13:13-14 (AMP)**

King Saul's outward disobedience revealed his inward heart condition. Through his actions, he demonstrated that he was rebellious against God, presumptuous concerning his priests, and lax toward the priorities of God's heart. In one swift moment, Saul disqualified himself from serving as king over God's people.

As a leader, you cannot lead the people God loves if you do not love the God that loves the people. Leaders must have a heart for God and in doing so, have a heart that loves what God loves. Unfortunately, Saul was not be able to serve God's people with the kind of heart that God desires.

> *"But the Lord said to Samuel, "Do not look at his appearance or at the height of his stature, because I have rejected him. For the Lord sees not as man sees; for man looks at the outward appearance, but the Lord looks at*

*the heart."* – **1 Samuel 16:7 (AMP)**

*"And when He had removed him, He raised up for them David as king, to whom also He gave testimony and said, 'I have found David the son of Jesse, a man after My own heart, who will do all My will."* - **Acts 13:22 (NKJV)**

God called David a man after his own heart giving him one of the highest compliments ever. At the time of David's anointing, God told Samuel that He looks at the heart while men look at the outward appearance. That means, God personally endorsed David because of his beautiful heart. Wow! It's one thing to be endorsed by another man but a completely different thing to be personally endorsed by God Almighty. What an honor to be known by God as a person who is after His heart and does everything He commands.

Unlike King Saul, David invested his time cultivating a heart filled with love, worship and willful surrender to God. That was evident through his prioritization of intimacy with God, humility in caring for his father's sheep and writing psalms of worship to God in the wilderness. David also understood the power of submission through his willful submission to God and the earthly authority God placed over his life.

<u>Never forget that it was David's heart that qualified him for the kingship, not his appearance, education, family background, or wealth.</u> Since that's the case it seems like cultivating your heart to submit to God is time well spent.

*"But the worries and cares of the world [the distractions of this age with its worldly pleasures], and the deceitfulness [and the false security or glamour] of wealth [or fame], and the passionate desires for all the other things creep in and choke out the word, and it becomes unfruitful."* – **Mark**

**4:19 (AMP)**

*"You were running a good race. Who cut in on you to keep you from obeying the truth?"* – **Galatian 5:7 (NIV)**

What are your distractions? Has your heart been drawn away from intimacy by the cares of this world? Has someone cut in on you and taken your eyes off Jesus? I have news for you. It's not too late to get a new heart.

*"Create in me a clean heart, O God, and renew a right and steadfast spirit within me."* – **Psalm 51:10 (AMP)**

If you ask, God will create a clean heart within you and renew your spirit so that living water can flow steadily from within you once again. Your answer from God is only a prayer away. Just ask.

❖ Now turn to Lesson Three in your companion **"One Month with A King: *Interactive Study Journal"*** to complete the corresponding GEM.

# ONE MONTH WITH A KING

# PART II
# PRODUCE IN REST

## INTRODUCTION

*"He gives power to the weak, and to those who have no might He increases strength. Even the youths shall faint and be weary, and the young men shall utterly fall, but those who wait on the LORD shall renew their strength; They shall mount up with wings like eagles, they shall run and not be weary, they shall walk and not faint."* -
**Isaiah 40:29-31 (NKJV)**

Waiting for God to fulfill His promise to use you can often feel like a tedious chore. Along the journey to fulfillment, God's vision for your life may seem unattainable and far from what you envisioned for yourself when you first accepted His call.

It can feel sometimes like the day He promised may never come. Also, the place that God has you in right now may seem like the last place to blossom because you feel hidden, even from God's eyes. Yet, you're right where you need to be and more importantly, you're right where God wants you to be.

In surveying the life of King David in Part II, you will discover the next three lessons and along the way, complete the corresponding activities in the companion **"One Month with A King: *Interactive Study Journal*"**:

 4. Bloom where you are planted
 5. Hiddenness is not Hopelessness
 6. God knows where to find you

## LESSON FOUR

## BLOOM WHERE YOU ARE PLANTED

*"Every time the commanders of the Philistines attacked, David was more successful against them than all the rest of Saul's officers. So, David's name became very famous."*
– **1 Samuel 18:30 (NLT)**

God is not interested in our well-thought-out plans and the path that we have mapped out to our pre-conceived destinations. He is interested in our journey along the path that is guided by His Word. There is so much He desires to do with us, in us, and through us, along the path that He has established for us to reach our destiny. I love the quote: *"It's not about the destination; it's about the journey."* This is a grand statement to make but can be an agonizing reality to walk out.

God is concerned about the process of making you into the image of His Son, Jesus Christ. It is a process that includes joy, adventure, blessings and new beginnings as well as, sorrow, mourning, loss, and healing past wounds. He will not stop until the perfect work He began in your life is fully completed. The various highs and lows of your journey are a part of the process of transformation into the beautiful image of Christ.

> *"For those whom He foreknew, He also predestined to become conformed to the image of His Son, so that He would be the firstborn among many brethren;"* –
> **Romans 8:29 (NASB)**
>
> *"Being confident of this very thing, that He who has begun a good work in you will complete it until the day of Jesus*

*Christ;"* - **Philippians 1:6 (NKJV)**

There is a book in heaven perhaps called "This Is Your Life", with your name on it. It's a beautiful story featuring YOU complete with a plot, setting, main characters, heroes, and of course, villains. It includes the day you were conceived, the intricate details of your woven body, your birthday, each day of your life, and the day you will die. Sobering when you think about it but reality, nevertheless.

> *"My frame was not hidden from You when I was made in secret, and skillfully wrought in the lowest parts of the earth. Your eyes saw my substance, being yet unformed. And in Your book they all were written, the days fashioned for me, when as yet there were none of them."* – **Psalm 139:15-16 (NKVJ)**

Wouldn't it be exciting to know which page of your life you were now on? What about all the juicy details surrounding the next chapter you are about to enter? How about the turn of events which await you three pages ahead? Regardless of the current page of your life's story, make the most of it. Acknowledge God's sovereignty and enjoy where you are along the journey. His plans for you are all for good and everything WILL work together for the good of His children who love Him and are called by Him (Rom. 8:28).

> *"That person is like a tree planted by streams of water, which yields its fruit in season and whose leaf does not wither-- whatever they do prospers"* - **Psalm 1:3 (NIV)**

> *"And we know that all things work together for good to those who love God, to those who are the called according to His purpose."* – **Romans 8:28 (NKJV)**

Since you know that God has a well-orchestrated plan for your life, you can confidently continue forward. Even when the road is long and seemingly impossible, you must surrender and allow God to perfect the work that He began in you. Quitting is not the answer. Instead, you must dig your heels in deeper, cling tighter to His hand and bloom where you are planted.

> *"God is our refuge and strength, a very present help in trouble. Therefore we will not fear, though the earth be removed, and though the mountains be carried into the midst of the sea; Though the waters thereof roar and be troubled, though the mountains shake with the swelling thereof. Selah."* - **Psalm 46:1-2 (NKJV)**

We were first introduced to David on the day that he was anointed to be king of Israel. By the time he was brought on the scene, he had already cultivated a heart that was fully after God. Once the Prophet Samuel anointed David, it was inevitable that he would become King and it was only a matter of time. Still, David could not foresee the journey or how long it would take before he ascended to the promised throne. Let's look at the account of the when Prophet Samuel anointed David as King:

> *"Now the LORD said to Samuel, "You have mourned long enough for Saul. I have rejected him as king of Israel, so fill your flask with olive oil and go to Bethlehem. Find a man named Jesse who lives there, for I have selected one of his sons to be my king." But Samuel asked, "How can I do that? If Saul hears about it, he will kill me." "Take a heifer with you," the LORD replied, "and say that you have come to make a sacrifice to the LORD. Invite Jesse to the sacrifice and I will show you which of his sons to anoint for me." So Samuel did as the LORD instructed. When he arrived at Bethlehem, the elders of the town came trembling to meet him. "What's wrong?" they asked. "Do you come in peace?" "Yes," Samuel replied. "I have come to sacrifice to the Lord. Purify yourselves and come with*

*me to the sacrifice." Then Samuel performed the purification rite for Jesse and his sons and invited them to the sacrifice, too. When they arrived, Samuel took one look at Eliab and thought, "Surely this is the LORD's anointed!" But the LORD said to Samuel, "Don't judge by his appearance or height, for I have rejected him. The LORD doesn't see things the way you see them. People judge by outward appearance, but the LORD looks at the heart." Then Jesse told his son Abinadab to step forward and walk in front of Samuel. But Samuel said, "This is not the one the LORD has chosen." Next Jesse summoned Shimea, but Samuel said, "Neither is this the one the LORD has chosen." In the same way all seven of Jesse's sons were presented to Samuel. But Samuel said to Jesse, "The LORD has not chosen any of these." Then Samuel asked, "Are these all the sons you have?" "There is still the youngest," Jesse replied. "But he's out in the fields watching the sheep and goats." "Send for him at once," Samuel said. "We will not sit down to eat until he arrives." So Jesse sent for him. He was dark and handsome, with beautiful eyes. And the LORD said, "This is the one; anoint him." So as David stood there among his brothers, Samuel took the flask of olive oil he had brought and anointed David with the oil. And the Spirit of the LORD came powerfully upon David from that day on. Then Samuel returned to Ramah." -* **1 Samuel 16:1-17 (NLT)**

It's easy to imagine that God's decision to choose David caused an "upset" in both the natural and spiritual realms. In the natural, his brothers probably lamented that David did not fit the perceived visual profile of a king. They may have tried to bully him for his lack of military experience and political incompetence. In the spirit realm, the angels and the great cloud of witnesses surely rejoiced.

David's name would eventually be known in the halls of

heaven as a radical worshipper, humble servant, and a lover of the Most High God. The enemy and all the hordes of hell knew of him also. They must have lamented the ascent of such an anointed warrior of God, from whose lineage God would bring forth the Messiah.

> *"Howbeit that was not first which is spiritual, but that which is natural; and afterward that which is spiritual."* -
> **1 Corinthians 15:46 (KJV)**

> *"And there shall come forth a rod out of the stem of Jesse, and a Branch shall grow out of his roots: And the spirit of the Lord shall rest upon him, the spirit of wisdom and understanding, the spirit of counsel and might, the spirit of knowledge and of the fear of the Lord;"* - **Isaiah 11:1-2 (NKJV)**

As glamorous as it may sound to be anointed as king, the path to David's destiny was filled with adversity, disappointment, pain, and hard work. His journey to the throne would take him on an unforeseeable path filled with twists and turns spanning several years. If God decided that David was the next king of Israel, why would the journey require him to face so many challenges? Why would it take so many years for David to realize the promise? What was David supposed to do in the meantime?

> *"Every time the commanders of the Philistines attacked, David was more successful against them than all the rest of Saul's officers. So, David's name became very famous."*
> **– 1 Samuel 18:30 (NLT)**

Interestingly, after David was anointed by Samuel, he returned to his role of tending the sheep. He did not shirk his responsibility. He remained faithful to his tasks, continued to worship in the wilderness, and humbly embraced his existing state of obscurity. However, I imagine that the promise of God daily gave him vitality as it burned vividly within his heart.

On the difficult and mundane days in the wilderness he learned to encourage himself in the Lord. He reflected often on God's promise regardless of his natural circumstances. In the relative inconspicuousness of his shepherding role, he did not allow impatience to drive him to vacate his position. Instead, he diligently served right where he was asked to be until the Lord sovereignly moved him into the next phase of his life.

We are not sure how much longer David remained in his role as a shepherd prior to his victory over Goliath (1 Sam. 17:51). However, we do know that it catapulted him into fame as Israel's "Giant Slayer". Soon after, the next phase of David's journey included fame, marriage, and a position as an officer in Saul's army.

Let's look at this account below;

> *"Now Michal, Saul's daughter, loved David. And they told Saul, and the thing pleased him. So Saul said, "I will give her to him, that she may be a snare to him, and that the hand of the Philistines may be against him." Therefore Saul said to David a second time, "You shall be my son-in-law today."* – **1 Samuel 18:20-21 (NKJV)**

> *Thus Saul saw and knew that the LORD was with David, and that Michal, Saul's daughter, loved him; and Saul was still more afraid of David. So Saul became David's enemy continually. Then the princes of the Philistines went out to war. And so it was, whenever they went out, that David behaved more wisely than all the servants of Saul, so that his name became highly esteemed.* – **1 Samuel 18:28-30 (NKJV)**

We see that despite Saul's growing jealousy, David continued to excel. Thus, David became captain of Saul's army and was sent on a "suicide" mission against the Philistines. Still, against all odds, David operated with wisdom and became known even more for his record of successful military victories. That made things even worse with King Saul. Though David was given a high position, Saul's motive was to set him up for failure. Yet instead of breaking under pressure, David performed brilliantly because the Lord was with him.

Often, the path to success and promotion is wrought with undesirable circumstances. It may be in the form of a difficult co-worker, hard to please supervisor, possessive church leader or some other negative experience. David's life serves as a model of how to remain at rest and still produce favorable results. We should rest in the knowledge that God will fulfill His promise and like David, while we wait, we can still produce.

To produce, while at rest, we should **occupy, demonstrate excellence, grow in competence, and remember God is the boss**.

❖ **Occupy until you see the promise.**

**The definition of occupy** is *"to engage the attention or energies of; to take up; to take or hold possession or control of; or to take or hold possession or control of" (Merriam Webster Open Dictionary)*.

When you have a promise from God, it's tempting to abruptly stop or press "pause" on the seemingly mundane activities of everyday life while you wait for it to come to pass. Yes, it is good to stand on the promises God has given for the future but do not stop what God has assigned you to complete in the present.

If God has given you an assignment to complete today, there is a high probability that it is to prepare you for the promise He has for you tomorrow. Perhaps, God wants you to develop transferable skills, build your character, or grow certain relationships while going through your current assignment. Therefore, seek to complete, acquire, and enjoy all that God has ordained for your life in the "**now**" season.

> *"He said therefore, A certain nobleman went into a far country to receive for himself a kingdom, and to return. And he called his ten servants, and delivered them ten pounds, and said unto them, Occupy till I come."* - **Luke 19:12-13 (KJV)**

❖ **Demonstrate an excellent work ethic.**

**Work ethic** is defined as *"a belief in work as a moral good: a set of values centered on the importance of doing work and reflected especially in a desire or determination to work hard" (Merriam Webster Open Dictionary).*

While you are waiting for the promise of God to come to pass, continue to complete your current role with excellence. It will position you for promotion and serve as a good testimony to unbelievers. Believe it or not, the world is watching Christians to see if we practice what we say we believe. Unfortunately, many have ruined their testimony through their negative words, attitudes, and actions. Even though you are expecting a transition, continuing to demonstrate excellence in your existing role shows that you are a person of integrity and character.

> *"Then this Daniel was preferred above the presidents and princes, because an excellent spirit was in him; and the king thought to set him over the whole realm."* - **Daniel 6:13 (KJV)**

# ONE MONTH WITH A KING

### ❖ Increase your competence.

**Competence** is defined as *"the quality or state of being competent; sufficiency of means for the necessities and conveniences of life; the knowledge that enables a person to speak and understand a language." (Merriam Webster Open Dictionary).*

While you are waiting for the promise of God to come to pass, you can sharpen and develop brand new skills. The Lord in His mercy may be giving you "strategic downtime" to increase your competency so you can excel even more. Time is one of your most valuable resources. Unlike finances and energy, once time is spent, it cannot be regenerated.

Therefore, invest your time in increasing your competency level in the important areas of your life. If you don't know where to start, start simple. You can complete a course, obtain a mentor, volunteer, and do research to increase your competence level better equipping you for where the Lord is taking you.

> *"Study to shew thyself approved unto God, a workman that needeth not to be ashamed, rightly dividing the word of truth."* - **2 Timothy 2:15 (KJV)**

### ❖ Submit to God's authority.

While you are waiting for the promise of God, do not forget that God is your boss. Whether you believe you have a reasonable or unreasonable supervisor, remember that the Lord is the One you ultimately work for. God is the one who promotes and places individuals in leadership. Therefore, your supervisor belongs to Him and will have to give an account to Him concerning you. God is also watching to see how you respond to the authority He has placed over you. Consequently, submit to the leaders that God has established because He is the ultimate authority.

> *"And whatsoever ye do, do it heartily, as to the Lord, and not unto men;* - **Colossians 3:23 (KJV)**

> *"Whatever your hand finds to do, do it with your might; for there is no work or device or knowledge or wisdom in the grave where you are going."* - **Ecclesiastes 9:10 (KJV)**

Whenever I faced difficult circumstances in high school, college, or at work I would call my dad for prayer and advice. After I poured out my lamentations concerning the circumstances, I expected an empathetic remark. Yet, my dad often responded by simply saying, "It's all a part of the training." This was not the response I was hoping to hear from him, but I understood exactly what he meant. Ninety-nine percent of the time, by the end of these difficult circumstances, I learned valuable lessons and gained important skills that God desired for me to attain.

Like David, your role is to rest in God and trust Him to direct you through each season. While you wait for the manifestation of His promise, you must bloom where you are planted. When you occupy, demonstrate excellence, increase your competence, and submit to God's authority you will bloom. Blooming where you are planted results in the development of foundational traits that will last a lifetime and favor with God and man.

The development of faithfulness, competence, discipline, character, and humility were imperative to David's success as king. Though he was anointed to be king in a moment, the journey to the throne took years. David was completely unaware of the long, difficult path that lay ahead. He never anticipated that he would contend with jealousy from his mentor, King Saul. As Saul's jealousy grew, he sent David on another deadly mission against the Philistines with the hopes of not returning.

> *"Then Saul said, "This is what you shall say to David: The king wants no dowry except a hundred foreskins of the Philistines, to take vengeance on the king's enemies.'" Now Saul's intention was to cause David's death at the hand of the Philistines."* – **1 Samuel 18:25 (AMP)**

In 1 Samuel 18, we see that instead of growing discouraged and dying on the mission, David excelled and was far more victorious than Saul ever imagined.

> *"David arose and went, he and his men, and killed two hundred Philistine men, and David brought their foreskins [as proof of death] and presented every one of them to the king, so that he might become the king's son-in-law. So Saul gave him Michal, his [younger] daughter, as a wife. When Saul saw and knew that the LORD was with David, and that Michal, his daughter, loved him, Saul was even more afraid of David; and Saul became David's constant enemy. Then the Philistine commanders (princes) came out to battle, and it happened as often as they did, that David acted more wisely and had more success than all Saul's servants. So his name was highly esteemed."* – **1 Samuel 18:27-30 (AMP)**

The journey to the promises of God for your life can be compared to an acorn that is planted in the ground. Wherever the seed is planted that is where it must derive its nutrients for each season of its development. Some seasons will be warm and refreshing while others will be cold and dry. Nevertheless, at the end of each season, the seed should have gleaned the nutrients necessary for it to grow into a fruitful tree. Hence, the role of the acorn is to remain planted, grow and bloom where it is located.

> *"He shall be like a tree planted by the rivers of water, that brings forth its fruit in its season, whose leaf also shall not wither; an whatever he does shall prosper."*- **Psalm 1:3 (NKJV)**

My husband affectionately calls me "Farmer Brown" because of my love for gardening. One lesson I have learned is that every soil type is able to sustain some form of plant life. There are six main soil categorizations based on the dominating size of the particulate composition (Boughton, 2017).

• Clay soils – These soils remain wet and cold in winter and dry out in summer (Boughton, 2017). These soils are difficult for gardening because they drain slowly but tend to dry out and crack in summer (Boughton, 2017). The plants that bloom beautifully in clay soils are *Hosta's, Iris' and Plantain Lilies*.

• Sandy soils – These soils are light, warm, dry and tend to be acidic and low in nutrients (Boughton, 2017). These soils have quick water drainage and are easy to work with. They are quicker to warm up in spring than clay soils but tend to dry out in summer and suffer from low nutrients (Boughton, 2017). The plants that bloom beautifully in sandy soils are *Black-eye Susan, Sage,* and *Collard Greens*.

• Silty soils – These soils are light, moisture retentive and have a high fertility rating (Boughton, 2017). Most species of plants can bloom well in silty soils including *Roses, Dogwood,* and *Flax*.

• Peaty soils – These soils consist of organic matter, moisture retentive and are an optimum base for planting (Boughton, 2017). The plants that bloom beautifully in peaty soils are *Tulips, Hibiscus,* and *Hummingbird Mint.*

- Chalky soils – These soils are highly alkaline due to the calcium carbonate or lime composition (Boughton, 2017). The plants that bloom beautifully in the chalky soil are *Chamomile, Echinacea,* and *Rudbeckia.*

- Loamy soils - These soils are a mixture of sand, silt, and clay and are fertile, easy to work with and provide good drainage (Boughton, 2017). The plants that bloom well in loamy soils are *Cucumbers, Onions,* and *Eggplant.*

Regardless of his position, David rested in The Lord and excelled along his journey to destiny. Like David, you can produce while at rest. No matter what kind of dirt you encounter on the road to destiny, choose to occupy, demonstrate excellence, increase your competence, and submit to God's authority. Embrace this season and bloom where you are planted!

- ❖ Now turn to Lesson Four in your companion **"One Month with A King: *Interactive Study Journal"*** to complete the corresponding GEM.

## LESSON FIVE

## HIDDENNESS IS NOT HOPELESSNESS

> *"One of the servants said to Saul, "One of Jesse's sons from Bethlehem is a talented harp player. Not only that— he is a brave warrior, a man of war, and has good judgment. He is also a fine-looking young man, and the Lord is with him."* - **I Samuel 16:7 (NLT)**

Are you currently in a situation where you feel like you're invisible? Do you feel like your kindness to family and friends is going unnoticed? Do you feel like you have been overlooked for a promotion at work? Do you feel like your faithfulness and service in your local church is unrecognized? Don't give up or lose hope. You may simply be in a God-ordained season of hiddenness. Here is how you can determine that.

Hopelessness is defined as *"having no expectation of good or success; despairing; not susceptible to remedy or cure; incapable of redemption" (Merriam Webster Open Dictionary).* Hiddenness is defined as *"concealed; obscure or covert" (Merriam Webster Open Dictionary).*

> *"Why are you in despair, O my soul? Why have you become restless and disquieted within me? Hope in God and wait expectantly for Him, for I shall yet praise Him, The help of my countenance and my God."* – **Psalm 42:11 (AMP)**

God in His infinite wisdom deals with His children according to times and seasons. Sometimes, when we seem forgotten by man, we perceive that we have been forgotten by God. Do not despair. The truth is that God's eyes are always on us and He is intimately acquainted with every season of our souls.

In His mercy, God will allow us to be hidden away from the worldly recognition to enable us to grow in integrity, build our character, and deepen our intimacy with Him. Though the Lord may have you in a purposeful season of hiddenness (Ecc.3:1), you are not without hope concerning His calling for your life (Ps. 42:11).

You can expect God to deliver on every prophetic and redemptive promise He has declared over you. Be encouraged! God knows exactly where you are, and He will unveil you to the world for His glory, at the right time.

> *"Now the Spirit of the LORD departed from Saul, and an evil spirit from the Lord tormented and terrified him. Saul's servants said to him, "Behold, an evil spirit from God is tormenting you. Let our lord now command your servants who are here before you to find a man who plays skillfully on the harp; and when the evil spirit from God is on you, he shall play the harp with his hand, and you will be well." So Saul told his servants, "Find me a man who plays well and bring him to me." One of the young men said, "Behold, I have seen a son of Jesse the Bethlehemite who is a skillful musician, a brave and competent man, a warrior, discerning (prudent, eloquent) in speech, and a handsome man; and the LORD is with him." So Saul sent messengers to Jesse and said, "Send me David your son, who is with the flock." Jesse took a donkey [loaded with] bread and a jug of wine and a young goat and sent them to Saul with David his son. Then David came to Saul and attended him. Saul loved him greatly and [later] David became his armor bearer. Saul sent word to Jesse, saying, "Please let David be my attendant, for he has found favor in my sight." So it came about that whenever the [evil] spirit from God was on Saul, David took a harp and played it with his hand; so*

*Saul would be refreshed and be well, and the evil spirit would leave him."* - **1 Samuel 16:14-23 (AMP)**

Early in the account of King Saul's disobedience in 1 Samuel 15, there was a sense that God's judgment was looming. Then Prophet Samuel declared the God had rejected King Saul and simultaneously found "a man after His own heart" as a fitting replacement. Consequently, even prior to Saul's rejection, in oblivion, David had already begun cultivating a fervent relationship with God. It was only a matter of time before God began putting into motion the circumstances of David's big reveal.

Whenever God removes one person from a place of prominence, He is always preparing a replacement in secret. While King Saul was aggressively seeking to preserve his personal kingdom, David was diligently worshipping and seeking God's kingdom. God is never caught off guard, unprepared, or short on provisions. In your hiddenness, you may be that very person He is preparing. So, lift your head, because with God, there is no place for hopelessness!

If David ever wavered in his duties or moved from his position during his season of obscurity, he might have missed his divine appointment. Guard your heart against offense while God teaches you patience and do not despise your season of waiting. That is when the transformation of your heart takes place.

> *"But the LORD said to Samuel, "Do not look at his appearance or at the height of his stature, because I have rejected him. For the LORD sees not as man sees; for man looks at the outward appearance, but the LORD looks at the heart."* – **1 Samuel 16:7 (AMP)**

God uses hiddenness as an incubator for greatness and the donning of beauty and that's reflected in nature.

## ONE MONTH WITH A KING

Throughout creation, we can see God's handwork perfected in secret. One perfect example is the development of the butterfly which undergoes a process called metamorphosis.

Metamorphosis is defined as *"a typically marked and more or less abrupt developmental change in the form or structure of an animal (such as a butterfly or a frog) occurring subsequent to birth or hatching" (Merriam Webster Open Dictionary).* This process requires a 28-38-day period of hiddenness. Let's look at one specific butterfly species as a quick case study. There are four distinct stages that the Monarch butterfly undergoes during the process of metamorphosis. These stages are the egg, larva, pupa, and adult.

The first stage of **metamorphosis** is the **egg phase**. This is the stage where the life of the butterfly begins. Though this tiny, nearly microscopic egg does not resemble a butterfly, hidden inside is the DNA to produce a full-grown butterfly. Once the metamorphic process has begun, the butterfly must see it all the way to completion. If the butterfly were to cease its development at any point during the process, it would die.

The second stage is the **larval phase**. At this stage of hiddenness, the larva (or caterpillar) emerges from the egg. For the duration of this phase, the caterpillar's sole purpose is to crawl from leaf to leaf just to eat and store nutrients. Though it has emerged from the egg, it still does not resemble a butterfly externally. To have emerged as a caterpillar is significant progress but, it is still far from the promise of an adult butterfly. If the caterpillar were to hopelessly cease its development at this stage, it would also die.

The caterpillar is not destined to remain at this phase. Nor is it equipped to survive the predators, terrain, and climatic changes beyond the designated length of this phase.

So, in hiddenness, the caterpillar feverishly spends its days eating, growing, and accumulating nutrients with the hope of progressing to the next stage of its transformation.

The third stage is the **pupa** or **chrysalis** phase. It is at this stage that the caterpillar reaches its maximum length and tissue capacity. As the developing caterpillar outgrows its external skin, its body hardens into a chrysalis. Despite its outward frozen appearance, hidden deep inside, the caterpillar is undergoing an intense transformation.

An inward battle ensues between the identity of the caterpillar and the butterfly. The pupa has transformed too much to remain a caterpillar, yet not far enough to emerge as a butterfly. For survival, the metamorphic process must be carried out to completion. Through internal struggle hidden away from external observation, its beautiful wings, vital organs, elongated limbs, and elegant face are developed.

The fourth stage is the **adult** or **butterfly** phase. At this final step of the process, the beautiful butterfly builds its strength up by struggling to emerge from its chrysalis exterior. If the butterfly does not persistently work to break through the chrysalis, it would still die at the final step of the process. Though inwardly, it is a butterfly, it now must outwardly learn how to maneuver like a butterfly.

Once free, the newly transformed butterfly must still wait patiently for the drying, extending, and functionality of its newly formed wings. This learning process is a vital part of its long-term survival. In the end, the adult butterfly would have completed the difficult process of metamorphosis and emerged from hiddenness. It would have traded its slow, crawling legs for fast, soaring wings.

*"Your servant has killed both the lion and the bear; and*

# ONE MONTH WITH A KING

*this uncircumcised Philistine will be like one of them, since he has taunted and defied the armies of the living God."* - **1 Samuel 17:36 (AMP)**

Like the butterfly, David spent his early years in hiddenness. His primary task was caring for sheep in the wilderness. He protected his sheep, even at the risk of death by a lion and bear. During this time of difficulty and struggle, David never faltered in his responsibility even though it seemed that his efforts were being ignored.

In the solitude, he diligently served and honored his earthly father by maintaining his post as a shepherd. At the same time, he honored his Heavenly Father through Psalms of worship. Though he was hidden, the Lord allowed Saul's servant to notice him and recommend him to serve in the palace.

*"Be still and know that I am God! I will be honored by every nation. I will be honored throughout the world"* - **Psalms 46:10 (NLT)**

If you are in a place of hiddenness, remain faithful and God will reveal you to the world in due season. Stay the course, faithfully serve and worship God with all your heart in the secret place and watch God reward you openly.

- ❖ Now, turn to Lesson Five in your companion **"One Month with A King: *Interactive Study Journal"*** to complete the corresponding GEM.

## LESSON SIX

## GOD KNOWS WHERE TO FIND YOU

*"Then Samuel asked, "Are these all the sons you have?" "There is still the youngest," Jesse replied. "But he's out in the fields watching the sheep and goats." "Send for him at once," Samuel said. "We will not sit down to eat until he arrives."*- **I Samuel 16:11 (NLT)**

Seasons come, and seasons go. In Christian life, there will be seasons when we are considered popular, admired, and well-liked. At the same time, our prayers get answered immediately, we experience promotion, and everything seems to be going our way.

However, there will also be seasons when we feel forgotten, despised, and even disliked by friends, family, and leaders. Simultaneously, the answers to our prayers may appear to be hindered, we're overlooked for promotion and nothing seems to be going according to plan. Life can be like that sometimes in this fallen world.

*"Be strong and courageous, do not be afraid or tremble at them, for the LORD your God is the one who goes with you. He will not fail you or forsake you"* – **Deuteronomy 3:16 (NASB)**

*"When you go through deep waters, I will be with you. When you go through rivers of difficulty, you will not drown. When you walk through the fire of oppression, you will not be burned up; the flames will not consume you"* - **Isaiah 43:2 (NLT)**

Which season are you in right now? Are you in one of

those difficult seasons? You must never forget that even though people might leave or forsake you, God has promised He never will. Despite the season you are in, there is comfort in knowing that God knows exactly where to **find you** because He is always **with you**.

You are never forgotten. God knows exactly where to find you when He is ready to use you. Let's look at some examples from scripture that align with difficult seasons and circumstances you will face one day or may be facing already.

**The Gideon Season - Insignificance**

> *"Now the Angel of the Lord came and sat under the terebinth tree which was in Ophrah, which belonged to Joash the Abiezrite, while his son Gideon threshed wheat in the winepress, in order to hide it from the Midianites. And the Angel of the Lord appeared to him, and said to him, "The Lord is with you, you mighty man of valor!" Gideon said to Him, "O my lord, if the Lord is with us, why then has all this happened to us? And where are all His miracles which our fathers told us about, saying, 'Did not the Lord bring us up from Egypt?' But now the Lord has forsaken us and delivered us into the hands of the Midianites." Then the Lord turned to him and said, "Go in this might of yours, and you shall save Israel from the hand of the Midianites. Have I not sent you?" So he said to Him, "O my Lord, how can I save Israel? Indeed my clan is the weakest in Manasseh, and I am the least in my father's house." And the Lord said to him, "Surely I will be with you, and you shall defeat the Midianites as one man."* **– Judges 6:11-16 (NKJV)**

Are you experiencing a season like Gideon? He was viewed as an insignificant member of his family. Yet, while hiding in fear from the Midianites, the Angel of the Lord found him. The Lord declared him to be a mighty man of valor, confirmed his calling and taught him how to lead armies into miraculous victories over the enemy.

## The Joseph Season – PIT (Prince in Training)

> *He sent a man before them— Joseph—who was sold as a slave. They hurt his feet with fetters, He was laid in irons. Until the time that his word came to pass, The word of the Lord tested him. The king sent and released him, The ruler of the people let him go free. He made him lord of his house, And ruler of all his possessions, To bind his princes at his pleasure, And teach his elders wisdom.* - **Psalm 105:17-22 (NKJV)**

Are you experiencing a season like Joseph? He found himself hidden away in dark pits and deep dungeons at the hands of those he trusted. He was betrayed by his brothers, falsely accused by his employer and imprisoned by his leader. While being stripped of his identity, sold into Egyptian slavery, and convicted as a common criminal, the Lord was with him. When the time was right, The Lord promoted, vindicated and used him to save the life of the same family members who rejected him and ultimately, the entire nation of Israel.

## The Paul and Silas Season - Persecution

> *"Then the multitude rose up together against them; and the magistrates tore off their clothes and commanded them to be beaten with rods. And when they had laid many stripes on them, they threw them into prison, commanding the jailer to keep them securely. Having received such a charge, he put them into the inner prison and fastened their feet in the stocks. But at midnight Paul and Silas were praying and singing hymns to God, and the prisoners were listening*

*to them. Suddenly there was a great earthquake, so that the foundations of the prison were shaken; and immediately all the doors were opened, and everyone's chains were loosed."* – **Acts 16:22-26 (NKJV)**

*"And he brought them out and said, "Sirs, what must I do to be saved?" So they said, "Believe on the Lord Jesus Christ, and you will be saved, you and your household." Then they spoke the word of the Lord to him and to all who were in his house. And he took them the same hour of the night and washed their stripes. And immediately he and all his family were baptized. Now when he had brought them into his house, he set food before them; and he rejoiced, having believed in God with all his household."*
– **Acts 16:30-34 (NKJV)**

Are you experiencing a season like Paul and Silas? They were savagely arrested, tortured and bound in the depths of a dark dungeon by religious authorities for preaching the gospel. During the darkest hour of their affliction, they sang melodious praise to God. Then, at midnight, both physical and spiritual prison doors were miraculously opened. Ultimately, their supernatural escape to physical freedom was not the biggest miracle of the night but the salvation and spiritual freedom of the keeper of the prison and his entire family.

### The Moses Season - Forgotten

*"Now it came to pass in those days, when Moses was grown, that he went out to his brethren and looked at their burdens. And he saw an Egyptian beating a Hebrew, one of his brethren. So he looked this way and that way, and when he saw no one, he killed the Egyptian and hid him in the sand... So Moses feared and said, "Surely this thing is known!" When Pharaoh heard of this matter, he sought to kill Moses. But Moses fled from the face of Pharaoh*

*and dwelt in the land of Midian; and he sat down by a well."* – **Exodus 2:11-12 & 15 (NKJV)**

*"Now Moses was tending the flock of Jethro his father-in-law, the priest of Midian. And he led the flock to the back of the desert, and came to Horeb, the mountain of God. And the Angel of the Lord appeared to him in a flame of fire from the midst of a bush. So he looked, and behold, the bush was burning with fire, but the bush was not consumed. Then Moses said, "I will now turn aside and see this great sight, why the bush does not burn. So when the Lord saw that he turned aside to look, God called to him from the midst of the bush and said, "Moses, Moses!" And he said, "Here I am. Then He said, "Do not draw near this place. Take your sandals off your feet, for the place where you stand is holy ground."* – **Exodus 3:1-5 (NKJV)**

*"Now therefore, behold, the cry of the children of Israel has come to Me, and I have also seen the oppression with which the Egyptians oppress them. Come now, therefore, and I will send you to Pharaoh that you may bring My people, the children of Israel, out of Egypt. But Moses said to God, "Who am I that I should go to Pharaoh, and that I should bring the children of Israel out of Egypt?"* – **Exodus 3:9-11(NKJV)**

Are you experiencing a season like Moses? Because of his crime of murder, he hid for forty years in the wilderness. It was a drastic step down from his position as a prince in Egypt. He felt inferior and disqualified to be used by the Lord. Then at the right time, The Lord spoke to him from a burning bush, commissioned him, and used him to miraculously lead the Children of Israel to freedom.

*"Then Moses said to the Lord, "O my Lord, I am not eloquent, neither before nor since You have spoken to Your*

*servant; but I am slow of speech and slow of tongue. So the anger of the Lord was kindled against Moses, and He said: "Is not Aaron the Levite your brother? I know that he can speak well. And look, he is also coming out to meet you. When he sees you, he will be glad in his heart. Now you shall speak to him and put the words in his mouth. And I will be with your mouth and with his mouth, and I will teach you what you shall do. So he shall be your spokesman to the people. And he himself shall be as a mouth for you, and you shall be to him as God. And you shall take this rod in your hand, with which you shall do the signs. Then Moses and Aaron did so; just as the Lord commanded them, so they did. And Moses was eighty years old and Aaron eighty-three years old when they spoke to Pharaoh.* – **Exodus 4:10, 14-17 & 7:7-8 (NKJV)**

*"Thus all the children of Israel did; as the Lord commanded Moses and Aaron, so they did. And it came to pass, on that very same day, that the Lord brought the children of Israel out of the land of Egypt according to their armies."* – **Exodus 12:50-15 (NKJV)**

You are never forgotten. Remember that God always knows exactly where to find you when He is ready to use you because He is always with you. God found Moses in the wilderness and he will find you.

Our hero, David started off hidden in the wilderness tending his father's flocks. On the day that Prophet Samuel visited Jesse's home, it is unclear if David was initially made aware of his arrival. Whether David was aware of the prophet's momentous visit or not, his father, Jesse was unconcerned that David was absent. While Samuel was in the house searching for the next king, David was carrying out his father's instructions in the fields watching over the sheep.

> *"Jesse had seven of his sons pass before Samuel. But Samuel said to Jesse, "The LORD has not chosen [any of] these." Then Samuel said to Jesse, "Are all your sons here?" Jesse replied, "There is still one left, the youngest; he is tending the sheep." Samuel said to Jesse, "Send word and bring him; because we will not sit down [to eat the sacrificial meal] until he comes here."* – **1 Samuel 16:10-11 (AMP)**

It is obvious that Jesse's chief concern was his seven older sons. He ensured that none of them missed the opportunity to potentially become Israel's next king. Jesse never intended to give David the chance that his older brothers had. However, we can rejoice that Jesse's plan did not deter God's plan.

> *But the LORD said to Samuel, "Do not look at his appearance or at the height of his stature, because I have rejected him. For the LORD sees not as man sees; for man looks at the outward appearance, but the LORD looks at the heart."* – **1 Samuel 16:7 (AMP)**

> *"And when He had removed him, He raised up David to be their king: of him He testified and said,* ***'I HAVE FOUND DAVID*** *the son of Jesse, A MAN AFTER MY OWN HEART [conforming to My will and purposes], who will do all My will."* – **Acts 13:22 (AMP) (emphasis mine)**

God was with David and His eyes were on David's heart. Even though Jesse preferred his older sons and Samuel was impressed by them, God rejected them all. Then, He required Jesse to summon his youngest son from the fields. David was brought to the forefront, publicly chosen by God and ceremoniously anointed to be king!

> *So he sent and brought him in. Now he was ruddy, with*

*bright eyes, and good-looking. And the Lord said, "Arise, anoint him; for this is the one!" Then Samuel took the horn of oil and anointed him in the midst of his brothers; and the Spirit of the Lord came upon David from that day forward. So Samuel arose and went to Ramah.* - **1 Samuel 16:12-13 (NKJV)**

In Acts 13:22, God declares that He FOUND David. You see, regardless of the season you are experiencing or the circumstances that may appear to be hiding you, God's eyes are always on you. Nothing is hidden from God's sight and there is no place that His omniscient presence can't reach you. Remember, God has not forgotten you. He knows where to find you because He is always with you.

*Where can I go from Your Spirit? Or where can I flee from Your presence?* – **Psalm 139:7 (NKJV)**

❖ Now, turn to Lesson Six in your companion **"One Month with A King: *Interactive Study Journal"*** to complete the corresponding GEM.

# ONE MONTH WITH A KING

# PART III
# REJECT REJECTION

# ONE MONTH WITH A KING

## INTRODUCTION

*But as for you, you meant evil against me; but God meant it for good, in order to bring it about as it is this day, to save many people alive.* – **Genesis 50:20 (NKJV)**

Along the way to fulfilling your calling, you will encounter varying degrees of opposition. The enemy will use many strategies to try and discourage, distract, delay, and even destroy the plans that God has for your life. One of the enemy's strategies is rejection, especially by fathers and other important authority figures.

We are not ignorant of the devil's schemes. He uses competitive jealousy, anger and insecurity to fuel the lie that we are rejected by everyone, including our Heavenly Father. That is a lie and the spirit of rejection must be rejected! We are not orphans. We can cry out to Abba Father, despite rejection by people. Our Father God has adopted us and accepted us as His children.

In surveying the life of King David in Part III, you will discover the next five lessons and along the way, complete activities in the companion "**One Month with A King: *Interactive Study Journal***".

7. Rejected by man, chosen by God
8. When earthly fathers fail us, God comes through
9. Success attracts jealousy
10. Spears will fly – Be prepared to duck
11. Cry out to Abba Father

## LESSON SEVEN

## REJECTED BY MAN, CHOSEN BY GOD

*"But the Lord said to Samuel, "Don't judge by his appearance or height, for I have rejected him. The Lord doesn't see things the way you see them. People judge by outward appearance, but the Lord looks at the heart." -* **1 Samuel 16:7 (NLT)**

Abraham Maslow was one of the most influential motivational theorists during the decade of 1940 - 1950. He developed a motivational needs theory that is famously known as Maslow's Hierarchy of Needs. Based on this motivational theory, human beings have five basic needs. His theory suggests that people behave in ways that best satisfy their needs according to a psychological needs hierarchy. They prioritize all their needs according to five key classification. These five needs consist of (1) physiological, (2) safety, (3) love and belonging, (4) esteem, and (5) self-actualization.

As human beings, we are motivated in ways that meet our higher-level needs once our lower-level needs have been met. For example, securing food, water, and shelter are considered higher priorities than the need for purchasing a new car. Food and water are physiological needs important for our survival. Shelter meets our basic need for safety and security.

The need for a new car, though it may serve a role in our safety, would probably fit in the category of esteem, especially, if we already own one that works just fine. Hence, only after the needs for food, water and shelter are met can pursing the new car may become the next motivator.

Right at the center of the hierarchy is the need for love and belonging or to "fit in". This need for belonging has been a key motivator within our Western society. This drives all cultural interactions, social media, corporate culture, relationship choices, fashions, and trends. When many of our biological, physiological and safety needs have been met, this need for love and belonging becomes the primary motivator. Unfortunately, we all know what it feels like to be "on the outside looking in.

**Who Rejected You?**

> *"For the world offers only a craving for physical pleasure, a craving for everything we see, and pride in our achievements and possessions. These are not from the Father, but are from this world."* - **1 John 2:16 (NLT)**

> *For we dare not class ourselves or compare ourselves with those who commend themselves. But they, measuring themselves by themselves, and comparing themselves among themselves, are not wise.* - **2 Corinthians 10:12(NKJV)**

The need for acceptance is innate in human nature. Regardless of race, ethnicity, class or culture, all people need a sense of belonging. People naturally want to associate themselves with other people. It's an important factor in how personal identities are shaped.

On the other hand, the direct antithesis of acceptance is rejection. It goes against human nature and is never a positive experience for the person on the receiving end of it. Rejection is defined as *"the act of not accepting, believing, or considering something: the state of being rejected" (Merriam Webster Open Dictionary).*

Sadly, rejection sometimes comes through the hands of people we trust the most. It is also a gateway to negative emotions and experiences like depression which can be weaponized by the devil to attack God's people. If you're dealing with depression as a result of rejection, the question for you today is, "Who rejected you?"

## A Family's Rejection

> *"When Joseph's brothers saw him coming, they recognized him in the distance. As he approached, they made plans to kill him. "Here comes the dreamer!" they said. "Come on, let's kill him and throw him into one of these cisterns. We can tell our father, 'A wild animal has eaten him.' Then we'll see what becomes of his dreams!"* – **Genesis 37:18-20 (NLT)**

> *Judah said to his brothers, "What will we gain by killing our brother? We'd have to cover up the crime. Instead of hurting him, let's sell him to those Ishmaelite traders. After all, he is our brother—our own flesh and blood!" And his brothers agreed. So when the Ishmaelites, who were Midianite traders, came by, Joseph's brothers pulled him out of the cistern and sold him to them for twenty pieces of silver. And the traders took him to Egypt.* – **Genesis 37:26-28 (NLT)**

Maybe you were rejected by your family. They may have felt that they did not want you or know how to love you well. The Bible has your situation covered. Joseph experienced rejection at the hands of his own brothers. Their jealousy even drove them to consider killing him. Instead, they made him a victim of human trafficking when they sold him into slavery. To conceal their crime, they deceived their father into believing that Joseph was killed by a wild animal.

## A Friend's Rejection

> *"And Simon Peter followed Jesus, and so did another disciple. Now that disciple was known to the high priest, and went with Jesus into the courtyard of the high priest. But Peter stood at the door outside. Then the other disciple, who was known to the high priest, went out and spoke to her who kept the door, and brought Peter in. Then the servant girl who kept the door said to Peter, "You are not also one of this Man's disciples, are you?" He said, "I am not." Now the servants and officers who had made a fire of coals stood there, for it was cold, and they warmed themselves. And Peter stood with them and warmed himself."* – **John 18:15-18 (NKJV)**

> *"Now Simon Peter stood and warmed himself. Therefore they said to him, "You are not also one of His disciples, are you?" He denied it and said, "I am not!" One of the servants of the high priest, a relative of him whose ear Peter cut off, said, "Did I not see you in the garden with Him?" Peter then denied again; and immediately a rooster crowed."* – **John 18:25-27 (NKJV)**

Maybe you were rejected by a friend. Perhaps someone you confided in and trusted betrayed you or abandoned you in a time of great need. You are not alone. Jesus knows exactly how you feel. He experienced rejection by most of his disciples after he was arrested in the Garden of Gethsemane.

What may have been the most disappointing to Jesus was the way in which Peter denied him three times in the darkest hours leading to the crucifixion. It's true that your friends can let you down when you need them to most. Jesus made it through and you can too.

**An Employer's Rejection**

*"Now Laban had two daughters: the name of the elder was Leah, and the name of the younger was Rachel. Leah's eyes were delicate, but Rachel was beautiful of form and appearance. Now Jacob loved Rachel; so he said, 'I will serve you seven years for Rachel your younger daughter. And Laban said, 'It is better that I give her to you than that I should give her to another man. Stay with me. So Jacob served seven years for Rachel, and they seemed only a few days to him because of the love he had for her. Then Jacob said to Laban, "Give me my wife, for my days are fulfilled, that I may go in to her. And Laban gathered together all the men of the place and made a feast. Now it came to pass in the evening, that he took Leah his daughter and brought her to Jacob; and he went in to her. And Laban gave his maid Zilpah to his daughter Leah as a maid. So it came to pass in the morning, that behold, it was Leah. And he said to Laban, "What is this you have done to me? Was it not for Rachel that I served you? Why then have you deceived me?" And Laban said, 'It must not be done so in our country, to give the younger before the firstborn. Fulfill her week, and we will give you this one also for the service which you will serve with me still another seven years. Then Jacob did so and fulfilled her week. So he gave him his daughter Rachel as wife also."* - **Genesis 29:16-28 (NKJV)**

Maybe you were rejected by an employer. Despite your hard work, dedication, and years of service you were denied a promised raise, back pay, promotion or growth opportunity. Jacob's employer Laban bamboozled him into marrying his daughter Leah after faithfully working for seven years. Then, instead of granting Jacob the hand of Rachel as promised, he required him to work an additional seven years.

**A Community's Rejection**

> *"There was a little city with few men in it; and a great king came against it, besieged it, and built great snares around it. Now there was found in it a poor wise man, and he by his wisdom delivered the city. Yet no one remembered that same poor man."* – **Ecclesiastes 9:14-15 (NKJV)**

> *"For if there should come into your assembly a man with gold rings, in fine apparel, and there should also come in a poor man in filthy clothes, and you pay attention to the one wearing the fine clothes and say to him, "You sit here in a good place," and say to the poor man, "You stand there," or, "Sit here at my footstool," have you not shown partiality among yourselves, and become judges with evil thoughts?"* – **James 2:2-4 (NKJV)**

Maybe you were rejected by your community. Regardless of your knowledge, understanding, expertise or experience you felt overlooked because of your socioeconomic status. That's a common theme in the scriptures. King Solomon told the story of a poor, wise man who provided a solution that delivered his city from destruction. However, because of his poverty, his wisdom and contribution to their salvation were quickly forgotten.

Thousands of years later, Jesus reiterated the importance of valuing people equally. Never let people's social or economic status be a differentiator in the way you treat them. The same way you don't want to feel the pain of being rejected by others in your community, try not to do the same to someone else.

### A Father's Rejection

Maybe you were rejected by your father. Tragically, rejection by fathers is a global epidemic. Rejection in this case comes in several different forms. Perhaps your father abandoned you or you never knew his identity. Perhaps your father was present, but he was emotionally absent, not supportive, or physically, emotionally, or sexually abusive.

You may even have experienced rejection from "father figures" such as stepfathers, pastors, community leaders, or mentors who failed you. According to an article by Focus on the Family, 24 million children live without their biological father in the home (Johnston, 2018, www.focusonthefamily.com).

The role of the father is to declare the identity of their sons and daughters (1 John 3:1). When fathers are absent, children are prone to spend their lives angry, wounded and searching for their identities. This rejection can also be projected onto God the Father, creating an obstacle to receiving His true love.

> *"And Samuel said to Jesse, "Are all the young men here?" Then he said, "There remains yet the youngest, and there he is, keeping the sheep. And Samuel said to Jesse, "Send and bring him. For we will not sit down till he comes here."*
> **– 1 Samuel 16:11 (NKJV)**

At home, David experienced rejection from his biological father, Jesse who assigned him to the dangerous task of defending sheep in the wilderness. Rejection of any kind can break the heart of a human being and derail them from their destiny. However, God is a Father to the fatherless, heals broken hearts, and lead them into their destiny!

> *"But the LORD said to Samuel, "Do not look at his appearance or at the height of his stature, because I have rejected him. For the LORD sees not as man sees; for man looks at the outward appearance, but the LORD looks at*

> *the heart."* – **1 Samuel 16:7 (AMP)**

> *"Then Samuel said to Jesse, "Are all your sons here?" Jesse replied, "There is still one left, the youngest; he is tending the sheep." Samuel said to Jesse, "Send word and bring him; because we will not sit down [to eat the sacrificial meal] until he comes here."* – **1 Samuel 16:11 (AMP)**

David was rejected by his father, brothers, and nearly by the Prophet Samuel early in his journey to becoming king of Israel. He experienced rejection from men before, during, and after being anointed. Upon Samuel's arrival, David's family never intended to invite him to join his brothers at the anointing ceremony. Before David was summoned, Prophet Samuel assumed God would choose one of David's older brothers instead.

> *"Now Eliab his oldest brother heard what he said to the men; and Eliab's anger burned against David and he said, "Why have you come down here? With whom did you leave those few sheep in the wilderness? I know your presumption (overconfidence) and the evil of your heart; for you have come down in order to see the battle."* – **1 Samuel 17:28 (AMP)**

You would think that after David was anointed to become king by the Prophet Samuel, his family would have been proud of him and demonstrated it. Yet, after David was officially anointed, the rejection continued. Right up until the moment he defeated Goliath, his brothers ridiculed him and marginalized his hard work as the family's shepherd.

> *"And, 'I will be a Father to you, and you will be my sons and daughters, says the Lord Almighty."*- **2 Corinthians 6:18 (NIV)**

*"When my father and my mother forsake me, then the Lord will take care of me."* – **Psalm 27:10 (NKJV)**

*"I will give you a new heart and put a new spirit within you; I will take the heart of stone out of your flesh and give you a heart of flesh. I will put My Spirit within you and cause you to walk in My statutes, and you will keep My judgments and do them."* – **Ezekiel 36:26-27 (NKJV)**

Despite all the rejection David experienced from his family members, he still became king over Israel. Remember, people judge using their eyes but only God looks at the heart (1 Samuel 16:7). Hence, you can be confident that God will never reject you and every promise He made to you, He will keep.

He will also heal your broken heart from the pain of rejection you may have experienced over the years (Ezekiel 36:26-27). Be encouraged! Even if your mother or father reject you, God will take you up (Psalm 27:10). He has not rejected you and never will!

❖ Now, turn to Lesson Seven in your companion **"One Month with A King: *Interactive Study Journal"*** to complete the corresponding GEM.

## LESSON EIGHT

## EARTHLY FATHERS MAY FAIL, OUR HEAVENLY FATHER WON'T

*"Now, my father, see! Indeed, see the edge of your robe in my hand! For in that I cut off the edge of your robe and did not kill you, know and perceive that there is no evil or rebellion in my hands, and I have not sinned against you, though you are lying in wait for my life to take it."* - **1 Samuel 24:11 (NASB)**

What image comes to mind when you think about your father? Is it an image of someone who has always been loving and kind? Is it an image of someone who has always been angry and cruel? Are your most memorable experiences with your father pleasant or unpleasant? Was your father your superhero? Do you know who he is? Was your father physically present but emotionally absent? Was he the one with the strong shoulder you could lean on during your most difficult experiences? Did your father abandon you? Did he set the high standard for manhood that you expect all men in your life to live up to?

People tend to project the image of their earthly fathers onto God, our Heavenly Father. Whether these images are good or bad, any comparison between God and an earthly father is inaccurate. Our Heavenly Father's love is perfect and there is no one like Him. He is always available to His children and never leaves them. God's word says *"…for the LORD your God goes with you; He will never leave you nor forsake you"* (Deut. 31:6 NIV). He is the perfect Father who never fails His children.

*"Though my father and mother forsake me, the LORD*

*will receive me." -* **Psalm 27:10 (NIV)**

*"Fathers, do not provoke your children to anger by the way you treat them. Rather, bring them up with the discipline and instruction that comes from the Lord." -* **Ephesians 6:4 (NLT)**

As a child, David may have experienced pain and rejection from his natural father, Jesse (Psalm 51:5). However, God allowed several other men to serve as father-figures to David at different times. This diverse company of individuals consisted of shepherds, priests, prophets, and kings. Though they were divinely given authority over David, at times, their fathering methods were deeply flawed.

*"But David said to Saul, "Your servant was tending his father's sheep. When a lion or a bear came and took a lamb out of the flock, I went out after it and attacked it and rescued the lamb from its mouth; and when it rose up against me, I seized it by its whiskers and struck and killed it." -* **1 Samuel 17:34-35 (AMP)**

*"I was brought forth in [a state of] wickedness; In sin my mother conceived me [and from my beginning I, too, was sinful]." –* **Psalm 51:5 (AMP)**

First, as the youngest son, David was the one assigned the dangerous task of protecting the family's sheep which included defending them against wild animals like lions and bears (1 Samuel 17:34). Perhaps, Jesse could have assigned this treacherous assignment to his older sons or provided David with a chaperone. By sending David into the wilderness alone, when he had seven older brothers, Jesse showed little concern for David's safety.

Also, the circumstances surrounding David's birth including the identity of his mother, or any background related to his conception may have been a little sketchy according to Psalm 51:5. It suggests that there may be a backstory that is not elaborated on in the scriptures. Though unclear, these dynamics point to the possibility that David held the status of "the family outcast".

> *"And Samuel said to Jesse, "Are all the young men here?" Then he said, "There remains yet the youngest, and there he is, keeping the sheep." And Samuel said to Jesse, "Send and bring him. For we will not sit down till he comes here." So he sent and brought him in. Now he was ruddy, with bright eyes, and good-looking. And the Lord said, "Arise, anoint him; for this is the one!" Then Samuel took the horn of oil and anointed him in the midst of his brothers; and the Spirit of the Lord came upon David from that day forward. So Samuel arose and went to Ramah.* – **1 Samuel 16:11-13 (NKJV)**

Second, David was not summoned by his father to initially stand with his brothers during Prophet Samuel's visit. After all his older brothers were presented before Samuel for consideration, Jesse acted like David didn't exist. However, after the prompting of the Lord, Samuel inquired about additional sons. This forced Jesse to summon David from the wilderness to join the event. Instead of proudly including David in the initial procession of his sons, Jesse needed to be nudged to get David.

> *"Look, my father! Indeed, see the hem of your robe in my hand! Since I cut off the hem of your robe and did not kill you, know and understand [without question] that there is no evil or treason in my hands. I have not sinned against you, though you are lying in wait to take my life."* – **1 Samuel 24:11 (AMP)**

Third, David spent several painful years of his life fleeing from one father-figure whose insecurity and fear concerning the loss of his throne could not be contained. King Saul's position enabled him to serve as a mentor to David. However, instead of seizing this divine opportunity to impart wisdom, experience, and guidance, Saul's interactions with David were harsh, wicked and offensive.

> *"Now David fled and escaped and came to Samuel at Ramah, and told him all that Saul had done to him. And he and Samuel went and stayed in Naioth."* - **1 Samuel 19:18 (NASB)**

Fourth, Prophet Samuel was a spiritual father-figure in David's life. He was the person who first anointed David, so he knew exactly where he came from and where he was going! Immediately after fleeing from King Saul's palace, David ran to the home of Prophet Samuel. Ironically, David did not run to his biological father, Jesse for support.

Instead, David knew that his spiritual father, Prophet Samuel would reassure, reaffirm, and remind him of who God called him to be. A good father is one who will reinforce the true identity of his children, declare life into them and pull greatness out of them. I can imagine that in David's distress while fleeing from Saul, Prophet Samuel pointed him to safety, prophesied life into him and reminded him of his destiny as king.

> *"Then Nathan said to David, "You are the man! Thus says the LORD, the God of Israel, 'I anointed you as king over Israel, and I spared you from the hand of Saul."* – **2 Samuel 12: 7 (AMP)**

> *"For whom the Lord loves He corrects, Just as a father the son in whom he delights."* - **Hebrews 3:12 (NKJV)**

Fifth and finally, the Prophet Nathan served as another spiritual father-figure for David. A good father understands the balance between encouragement and correction. When his children do things right, he knows that they need praise, but then they do things wrong, he knows that they need correction. Prophet Nathan did that for King David. Fortunately, when Prophet Nathan confronted the King about his sin with Bathsheba, David was quick to repent. Because of this stern confrontation, David was convicted of sin and returned to fellowship with God the Father.

A good father should not only encourage and support his children but provide honest and stern discipline when needed. Discipline is appropriate under the right circumstances and should always be motivated by love, to stimulate positive change. Even God says He disciplines His children because He loves them.

On the other hand, a father's failure to correct his children when they are in error amounts to neglect, which demonstrates a lack of love or concern for their future well-being. Prophet Nathan corrected David when he was in error. His failure to do so would have facilitated further harm to David's life and his overall relationship with God. Instead, Nathan's correction was well received and prompted David's repentance which led to the rededication of his life to God.

> *"Look, I am sending you the prophet Elijah before the great and dreadful day of the Lord arrives. His preaching will turn the hearts of fathers to their children, and the hearts of children to their fathers. Otherwise I will come and strike the land with a curse."* - **Malachi 4:5-6 (NLT)**

God will purposely place fathers in our lives to train, direct, and guide us into our destinies. The hope is that they will choose to father us well and when they do, we will choose to submit to their leadership. Bad experiences with earthly fathers can distort our image of God as our Heavenly Father. It can also cause us to lose confidence and hope for a successful future. However, this was not the case for David. Despite his various experiences with earthly fathers, He consistently enjoyed a positive, vibrant, worshipful relationship with God the Father.

David maintained a healthy image of his Heavenly Father because he developed a personal relationship with God that was completely separate from any earthly relationship. God is a good Father and He is unlike any earthly father we have ever known. Ask the Lord to reveal and heal any areas of pain that you have experienced with your earthly fathers. He is waiting, willing, and able to heal you everywhere that you hurt. If David's relationship with His Heavenly Father thrived despite the failures of his earthy fathers, you can do the same. God is right where you are. He promised to never leave nor forsake you so don't let anyone on earth cause you to leave or forsake Him.

- ❖ Now, turn to Lesson Eight in your companion **"One Month with A King: *Interactive Study Journal"*** to complete the corresponding GEM.

## LESSON NINE

## SUCCESS ATTRACTS JEALOUSY

*"This made Saul very angry. "What's this?" he said. "They credit David with ten thousands and me with only thousands. Next they'll be making him their king!" -* **1 Samuel 18:8 (NASB)**

*Anger is cruel, and wrath is like a flood, but jealousy is even more dangerous. -* **Proverbs 27:4 (NLT)**

Merriam Webster (2016), defines jealousy as *"an unhappy or angry feeling of wanting to have what someone else has."* Jealousy is jokingly referred to as the "green-eyed monster" that has the persona of being mild and cuddly. It is not a mythical monster, but a furious spirit that is anything but mild and cuddly. The spirit of jealousy is violent and unquenchable, and hard to stand against.

*"For wherever there is jealousy and selfish ambition, there you will find disorder and evil of every kind" -* **James 3:16 (NLT)**

If you open your heart to jealousy that is only the beginning of a destructive process. Jealousy is hardly ever alone. It is often accompanied by slander, murder, strife, division and a host of other wicked activities. The scripture clearly states this. God hates the spirit of jealousy. It is the same spirit that resulted in Lucifer being cast down from heaven.

*"For you said to yourself, 'I will ascend to heaven and set my throne above God's stars. I will preside on the*

*mountain of the gods far away in the north."* – **Isaiah 14:13 (NLT)**

Satan loves to use the spirit of jealousy to cause infighting, competition, and strife among friends, families, co-workers, church members and all types of leadership. His age-old strategy is to "divide and conquer". This demonic spirit manifests in many different forms including the spreading of vicious rumors, gossip, slander and blatant lies. It also displays itself as disrespectful manners, harsh words, negative attitudes, and adverse behaviors toward peers or authorities.

It is even demonstrated by silent hostile undertones, unspoken rivalries or flaunting of one's accomplishments in an effort to "one-up" the accomplishments of another. This spirit is lethal because wherever it is in operation, there is no limitation to the depths of darkness that accompany it. There's no way to contain jealousy. If it's there, it will only grow.

> *"Who is wise and understanding among you? By his good conduct let him show his works in the meekness of wisdom. But if you have bitter jealousy and selfish ambition in your hearts, do not boast and be false to the truth. This is not the wisdom that comes down from above, but is earthly, unspiritual, demonic. For where jealousy and selfish ambition exist, there will be disorder and every vile practice."* – **James 3:13-16 (ESV)**

Jealousy is a master of disguise. Sadly, I have experienced how the enemy easily can use the spirit of jealousy to turn those whom I believed were for me, completely against me. I have found that this spirit often hides behind insincere smiles, flattering lips, lavish gifts, hugs, and perceived holy kisses. Therefore, we must rely on the Holy Spirit to give us keen discernment to navigate through our relationships.

Satan exploits the insecurity of jealous people causing them to feel inferior, overly sensitive and offended. At the same time, the people of whom they are jealous may not understand the cause nor can these people provide the cure for their bitter counterparts.

This wicked spirit can destroy families, businesses, civic organizations and ministries. Unfortunately, jealousy arises at the most inopportune time when someone covets the success, possessions, attributes or position of someone else who is simply doing what's right. This is truly heartbreaking for an unsuspecting victim of jealousy and breaks the heart of God.

> *"Then this Daniel distinguished himself above the governors and satraps, because an excellent spirit was in him; and the king gave thought to setting him over the whole realm. So the governors and satraps sought to find some charge against Daniel concerning the kingdom; but they could find no charge or fault, because he was faithful; nor was there any error or fault found in him. Then these men said, "We shall not find any charge against this Daniel unless we find it against him concerning the law of his God."* – **Daniel 6:3-5 (NKJV)**

Daniel encountered the spirit of jealousy throughout his life because he had an "excellent" spirit. Wherever you find someone operating in the spirit of excellence, you can expect the spirit of jealousy to try and stop them. Think about it a little. Why did the other leaders hate Daniel with such evil passion? He operated in excellence. That's it. Even when they tried, they could find nothing wrong with him. That's why jealousy is both illogical, unfair and completely evil and people on the receiving end of it are victims.

> *"Then there arose a dispute between some of John's*

*disciples and the Jews about purification. And they came to John and said to him, "Rabbi, He who was with you beyond the Jordan, to whom you have testified—behold, He is baptizing, and all are coming to Him!" John answered and said, "A man can receive nothing unless it has been given to him from heaven. You yourselves bear me witness, that I said, 'I am not the Christ,' but, 'I have been sent before Him.' He who has the bride is the bridegroom; but the friend of the bridegroom, who stands and hears him, rejoices greatly because of the bridegroom's voice. Therefore this joy of mine is fulfilled. He must increase, but I must decrease."* – **John 30:25-30 (NKJV)**

When you are confident in who you are in Christ and the unique purpose He has for you, you will not be jealous of anyone else. John the Baptist had the opportunity to become jealous of Jesus when the people who once followed him, began following Jesus instead. John did not take the bait to accept the spirit of jealousy. Instead, he understood the unique purpose God gave him to prepare the way for Jesus until He arrived. Once Jesus came on the scene, John accepted that the spotlight had to shift away from him unto Jesus. Thus, he genuinely rejoiced as the crowds began engaging with Jesus, their Messiah.

*"So David went out wherever Saul sent him, and he acted wisely and prospered; and Saul appointed him over the men of war. And it pleased all the people and also Saul's servants. As they were coming [home], when David returned from killing the Philistine, the women came out of all the cities of Israel, singing and dancing, to meet King Saul with tambourines, [songs of] joy, and musical instruments. The women sang as they played and danced, saying, "Saul has slain his thousands, and David his ten thousands."* – **1 Samuel 18:5-7 (AMP)**

Our hero, David loved the Lord and every task he was

given he faithfully completed as unto The Lord (Acts 13:22). When Saul appointed him over the army, he excelled by killing far more enemies than Saul himself had ever done. Eventually, David's accomplishments gained the attention of the city to the degree that great war songs were written about him.

> *"Then Saul became very angry, for this saying displeased him; and he said, "They have ascribed to David ten thousands, but to me they have ascribed [only] thousands. Now what more can he have but the kingdom?" Saul looked at David with suspicion [and jealously] from that day forward. Now it came about on the next day that an evil spirit from God came forcefully on Saul, and he raved [madly] inside his house, while David was playing the harp with his hand, as usual; and there was a spear in Saul's hand. Saul hurled the spear, for he thought, "I will pin David to the wall." But David evaded him twice. Now Saul was afraid of David, because the LORD was with him, but had departed from Saul. So Saul had David removed from his presence and appointed him as his commander of a thousand; and he publicly associated with the people. David acted wisely and prospered in all his ways, and the LORD was with him. When Saul saw that he was prospering greatly, he was afraid of him. But all Israel and Judah loved David, because he publicly associated with them.* – **1 Samuel 18:8-16 (AMP)**

David's continuous success intimidated Saul and the spirit of jealousy caused him to despise David. King Saul feared that David would take his kingdom and rightfully so. Though David tried to console and reassure Saul of his love as a spiritual son, the spirit of jealousy and competition drove Saul to spend the rest of his life trying to kill David. Saul's quest to destroy David cost him everything. He ultimately lost his sanity, family, and life in his pursuit of David, God's chosen King of Israel.

# ONE MONTH WITH A KING

Be aware that the spirit of jealousy will try to come against you as you strive to for excellence in all that you do before God. At the same time, be on guard as the spirit of jealousy may subtly manipulate you into being jealous of someone else. Therefore, search your heart and repent if even a hint of jealousy can be found within you for someone else. Don't give room in your heart to the devil. Remember, success attracts jealousy. You're either going to be successful and be the object of jealousy or you're going to be jealous of someone else's success. The choice is yours.

❖ Now, turn to Lesson Nine in your companion **"One Month with A King: *Interactive Study Journal"*** to complete the corresponding GEM.

## LESSON TEN

## SPEARS WILL FLY, BE PREPARED TO DUCK

> *"...But Saul had a spear in his hand, and he suddenly hurled it at David, intending to pin him to the wall. But David escaped him twice."* - **1 Samuel 18:10-11 (NLT)**

In Psalms 91, God promised that we would not need to fear terror by night nor the arrow that flies at noonday (Psalm 91:5). The word "terror" refers to *extreme fear, dread or horror*. When you think of terror, darkness and evil may come to mind. It causes that anxious feeling while walking through unsafe streets, dark alleys or dangerous territory. The word "arrow" refers to *a shaft sharpened at the front and with feathers or vanes at the back, shot from a bow as a weapon or for sport"*. When you think of arrows, a sharp object flying unexpectedly, may come to mind.

> *"He will cover you and completely protect you with His pinions, and under His wings you will find refuge; His faithfulness is a shield and a wall. You will not be afraid of the terror of night, nor of the arrow that flies by day,"* – **Psalm 91:4-5 (AMP)**

> *"For He will command His angels in regard to you, to protect and defend and guard you in all your ways [of obedience and service]."* – **Psalm 91:11 (AMP)**

Like terrors at night and arrows in the day, you will encounter both expected and unexpected attacks at various times of your life. There will be times when you will know exactly where and when to expect trouble. There will also be times when offensive words or actions will come from people, places and at times that are completely unexpected. Look closely at the words of the psalmist in Psalm 91:5. He never said there **wouldn't be** terrors at night or arrows that fly during the day. He said that we do not have to **fear** them and that God would **protect** us.

> *"Above all, lift up the [protective] shield of faith with which you can extinguish all the flaming arrows of the evil one."* – **Ephesians 6:16 (AMP)**

> *"No temptation [regardless of its source] has overtaken or enticed you that is not common to human experience [nor is any temptation unusual or beyond human resistance]; but God is faithful [to His word—He is compassionate and trustworthy], and He will not let you be tempted beyond your ability [to resist], but along with the temptation He [has in the past and is now and] will [always] provide the way out as well, so that you will be able to endure it [without yielding, and will overcome temptation with joy]."* - **1 Corinthians 10:13 (AMP)**

In Ephesians 6:16, Apostle Paul identified the source of the flaming arrows that are launched toward the Children of God; the evil one. His arrows are unleashed to challenge our faith and they can come from anywhere. Yet, we do not need to fear them because the Lord is with us. He protects us and provides ways to escape the same way David escaped Saul's spear.

On two occasions, David ducked to avoid being killed by the spear or large arrow that Saul lunged at him (1 Samuel 18:11 & 1 Samuel 19:10). I am sure David was shocked when he saw Saul's arrow hurling through the air in his direction. An attack like that from the king was completely unexpected. Until then, he viewed Saul as a trusted father and mentor who had his best interest at heart. David had to come to the painful realization that his life was in danger at the hands of a person he deeply loved and trusted.

> *"For it was not an enemy that reproached me; then I could have borne it: neither was it he that hated me that did magnify himself against me; then I would have hid myself from him: But it was thou, a man mine equal, my guide, and mine acquaintance. We took sweet counsel together, and walked unto the house of God in company."* - **Psalm 55:12-14 (KJV)**

> *"…This is what the LORD says: Do not be afraid! Don't be discouraged by this mighty army, for the battle is not yours, but God's."* - **2 Chronicles 20:15 (NLT)**

Instead of retaliating, David chose to allow the Lord to fight his battle. This is a vital lesson for us because, when faced with opposition, we are often tempted to seek retribution for the pain we endure. I have discovered that it is hard for people to withhold retaliation when an offense is committed against them by a stranger but much harder when the offender is a trusted friend, brother, spouse, or leader.

> *"So David departed from there and escaped to the cave of Adullam; and when his brothers and all his father's house heard about it, they went down there to him."* – **1 Samuel 22:1 (AMP)**

> *"So David fled and escaped and came to Samuel at Ramah, and told him everything that Saul had done to him. And he and Samuel went and stayed in Naioth."* – **1 Samuel 19:18 (AMP)**

> *"But David said in his heart, "Now I will die one day by the hand of Saul. There is nothing better for me than to escape to the land of the Philistines. Then Saul will give up searching for me inside the borders of Israel, and I will*

*escape from his hand [once and for all]."* – **1 Samuel 27:1 (AMP)**

Those who are done wrong feel that they must retaliate to regain their respect and reestablish their self-worth. Yet, David resisted this temptation to retaliate against King Saul, by simply ducking out of the way and escaping. Along his journey to becoming king, David also had to duck into caves (1 Samuel 22:1), duck into Prophet Samuel's house (1 Samuel 19:18), and even duck into the camp of the Philistines (1 Sam. 27:1) to escape King Saul. Like David, God will protect each of us from the fiery darts of the enemy by providing ways of escape if we must choose to use them.

> *"There hath no temptation taken you but such as is common to man: but God is faithful, who will not suffer you to be tempted above that ye are able; but will with the temptation also make a way to escape, that ye may be able to bear it"* - **1 Corinthians 10:13 (KJV)**

The Lord provided multiple ways of escape for David as he fled from the arrows of his enemy. If David did not choose to duck, he would have been wedged right between King Saul and God's wrath. Instead of King Saul receiving his punishment for his offenses, David would have borne the brunt of God's judgment because he would have been in the way. When you're under attack, you will miss the way of escape if you allow your emotions to cause you to get in God's way and retaliate against your offenders. You must predetermine in our heart to duck when spears are launched in your direction and allow God to fight for you.

Here's how you predetermine to duck when offense comes your way. You must purpose to forgive immediately and release your offenders to God. If you do not purpose in your heart to restrain yourself before unexpected offenses arise, you will not remember to restrain yourself in the actual moment it happens.

Accordingly, allow me to reinforce the point with this closing thought. When you are faced with arrows flying in your direction unexpectedly, DUCK! Forgive, pray for your offenders and look for God's provided escape route, then stay out of His way as He executes judgment. He always provides a way of escape so that He can fight on your behalf. Isn't that good news? The Lord will fight your battles. Just **be prepared to duck** out of the way!

❖ Now, turn to Lesson Ten in your companion **"One Month with A King: *Interactive Study Journal"*** to complete the corresponding GEM.

## LESSON ELEVEN

## CRY OUT, ABBA FATHER

> *"In my distress I called upon the LORD, and cried to my God for help; He heard my voice out of His temple, and my cry for help before Him came into His ears."* – **Psalm 18:5 (NASB)**

Who do you call when you are in distress? Do you immediately run to God the Father in prayer or do you pick up the phone and call someone to lament over your problems? We would all like to say that our first response is to quickly cry out to our Heavenly Father in prayer. However, we know this is not always the case. When our backs are against the wall, we respond by doing what we know. Although it is acceptable to call on a trusted brother or sister in our time of need, we should appeal to Abba Father first.

> *"The Spirit…brought about your adoption to sonship. And by him we cry, "Abba, Father."* - **Romans 8:15 (NIV)**

In our frailty, too often our first response is to cry out to a fellow human being who may be able to offer support, but not a solution. Sadly, many of our well-meaning acquaintances will give us advice that is either incomplete, inaccurate, or ineffective. Their advice may be limited in scope or skewed by their relationship history with us, knowledge of the subject matter, personal experiences, emotional state, social environment, individual perspective and inadequate reasoning.

These factors interfere with their ability to provide us

with comprehensive, accurate solutions. For many of us, by the time we finally go to God for answers, we have taken the advice of others and made a bad situation worse. Additionally, bad advice endangers good relationships. It's easy to get offended when you take the advice of a friend and it doesn't work.

At the same time, when a fellow Christian approaches you for advice, it is wise to first ask this key question; *"What do you feel The Lord is saying to you concerning this situation?"* This is important because this question should prompt any Christian to pray. If the person is struggling to hear from God, offer to pray first, before offering advice. If the person has already prayed, he/she should be able to share The Lord's instructions with you. You can then both go to the scriptures together to confirm the Word of the Lord.

Keep this in mind. Though your heart is to help the person, do not rush to offer advice based on your limited understanding. It's better to listen, empathize and be slow to speak. This is especially important when someone is seeking advice from you concerning a family-related issue. How you respond can prove to be detrimental to your relationship with the person in the long-run. In your eagerness to help someone through a domestic issue, your sincere efforts could backfire. Why? Once the family issue is resolved, the parties involved could potentially "close ranks" and turn against you because your response was perceived as taking sides.

> *"God is our refuge and strength [mighty and impenetrable], a very present and well-proved help in trouble."* – **Psalm 46:1 (AMP)**

Our Heavenly Father has promised to answer us and be our help in our time of need. We are His children. He is willing and more than able to deliver us from all our troubles. I know that many of us know this, but do we truly believe this? Do our actions in times of distress align with what we say we believe concerning the sovereignty of Almighty God and His tremendous ability to deliver us?

David honestly knew, believed, and demonstrated it with actions. His faith was rock-solid. When he was surrounded by mighty men, priests, and prophets he knew that Abba Father was the only one who could deliver him. Accordingly, when he was alone, he was able to trust God just the same.

David ran for his life from Saul then later from his own son, Absalom, but he always knew where to turn. He cried out to his Heavenly Father and believed that He would answer. Throughout those difficult seasons of his life's journey, he penned many psalms of heartfelt prayers to God. As a good Father, God responded to his son, David by delivering him from Saul, Absalom, and every other foe. In Psalm 18, David expressed his love, faith, and praise to God for hearing his cry.

> *"I will love You, O LORD, my strength. The LORD is my rock and my fortress and my deliverer; My God, my strength, in whom I will trust; My shield and the horn of my salvation, My stronghold. I will call upon the LORD, who is worthy to be praised; So shall I be saved from my enemies. The pangs of death surrounded me, And the floods of ungodliness made me afraid. The sorrows of Sheol surrounded me; The snares of death confronted me. In my distress I called upon the LORD, And cried out to my God; He heard my voice from His temple, And my cry came before Him, even to His ears"* - **Psalm 18:1-6 (NKJV)**

- ❖ Now, turn to Lesson Eleven in your companion **"One Month with A King: *Interactive Study***

*Journal"* to complete the corresponding GEM.

# PART IV
# BRACE FOR BATTLE

# ONE MONTH WITH A KING

## INTRODUCTION

*"And he said, "Listen, all Judah and the inhabitants of Jerusalem and King Jehoshaphat: thus says the LORD to you, 'Do not fear or be dismayed because of this great multitude, for the battle is not yours but God's."* – **2 Chronicles 20:15 (NASB)**

The fulfillment of your calling will not come without a fight because you have a real enemy. The great news is, he is powerless to stop the plan of God. God will fight your battles. However, for the victory to be fully realized, you must come into agreement with God and follow all His instructions. So brace for battle by embracing God's uncommon training strategies. Put on the armor of God and transform your mind with the Word of God.

In surveying the life of King David in Part IV, you will discover the next five lessons and along the way, complete activities in the companion "**One Month with A King: *Interactive Study Journal*"**.

12. Don't flee – Advance toward your enemy
13. Uncommon victories require uncommon training
14. God alone can cast the first stone
15. Invisible armor – Invincible God
16. Avoid imagination exaggeration

# ONE MONTH WITH A KING

## LESSON TWELVE

## DON'T FLEE, ADVANCE TOWARD YOUR ENEMY

> *"Then it happened when the Philistine rose and came and drew near to meet David, that David ran quickly toward the battle line to meet the Philistine."* - **1 Samuel 17:48 (NASB)**

What do you do when you are faced with adversity? Do you run and hide or do you face it head on? As a Child of God, you do not have to be afraid when the enemy comes against you. Still, the scripture reminds you to *"be sober, be vigilant; because your adversary the devil walks about like a roaring lion, seeking whom he may devour."* (1 Peter 5:8 NKJV)

> *"So shall they fear the name of the LORD from the west, and his glory from the rising of the sun. When the enemy shall come in like a flood, the Spirit of the LORD shall lift up a standard against him."* - **Isaiah 59:19 (KJV)**

God has equipped you with the Word of God to advance in battle and route the enemy. Therefore, be bold and know that no weapon formed against you will prosper (Joshua 1:9 & Isaiah 54:17). You only need to declare the Word of God in faith, stand firm in your God-given authority, and watch your enemy flee.

> *"Have I not commanded you? Be strong and courageous! Do not be terrified or dismayed (intimidated), for the LORD your God is with you wherever you go."* - **Joshua 1:9 (AMP)**

> *"No weapon that is formed against you will succeed; and*

*every tongue that rises against you in judgment you will condemn. This [peace, righteousness, security, and triumph over opposition] is the heritage of the servants of the Lord, and this is their vindication from Me," says the Lord." -* **Isaiah 54:17 (AMP)**

*"Submit yourselves therefore to God. Resist the devil, and he will flee from you." -* **James 6:7 (KJV***)*

One of my favorite pastimes is watching animal documentaries. Recently, I watched one featuring Appalachian Mountain goats. They are the largest mammals found in high-altitude mountainous locations with elevations of 13,000 feet (4,000 m) or more. They are completely covered with long, wooly, all-white fur and possess two short, slender, black horns. Even with these horns, they are somewhat defenseless against direct contact with large predators. Yet, the mountainous terrain they live on serves as their primary line of defense. Their padded black hooves equip them with the uncanny ability to be nimble in the most rigorous topography. Also, because they can remain high on the mountains, they are keenly aware of their enemies approaching from below and can prepare to defend themselves before contact.

On the program I watched, a large, powerful cougar unexpectedly scaled the steep mountain and cornered a small, defenseless mountain goat. Just when I thought the goat was about to be devoured, instead of running, the goat lowered its sharp horns and aggressively advanced toward its enemy. It then dodged the cougar's large paws and sharp teeth by skillfully advancing, gripping the ledge and rapidly thrusting its sharp horns into the cat. The goat's advancement strategy, coupled with the high elevation and slippery ledge caused the cougar to retreat.

At that point, the mountain goat effortlessly leaped to

higher elevations on the treacherous mountain side. I laughed in amazement.

> *"He maketh my feet like hinds' feet, and setteth me upon my high places."* – **Psalm 18:33 (KJV)**

In the documentary I watched, the mountain goat's surefooting on the mountain enabled it to skillfully use its sharp horns to advance against its much bigger, stronger enemy at high elevations. That's a picture of spiritual warfare. Like the mountain goat, we must remain high on the mountain of God because that is our position of power. Abiding in Him and His Word enables us to advance toward the enemy. He has promised to give us hind's feet so that we can remain stable in high places with Him.

> *"Put on salvation as your helmet, and take the sword of the Spirit, which is the word of God."* – **Ephesians 6:14 (NLT)**

> *"He has made My mouth like a sharp sword, In the shadow of His hand He has concealed Me; And He has also made Me a select arrow, He has hidden Me in His quiver."* – **Isaiah 49:2 (NASB)**

> *"From his mouth came a sharp sword to strike down the nations. He will rule them with an iron rod. He will release the fierce wrath of God, the Almighty, like juice flowing from a winepress."* - **Revelation 19:15 (NLT)**

Too often, Christians retreat when they sense even the slightest hint of an attack from the enemy. Let that not be said of you. What attacks have the enemy launched against you? As a Child of God, you do not have to take his attacks lying down. When the enemy attacks in a particular area of your life, you should be ready to declare the Word of God concerning that specific situation. Instead of retreating in fear, you must run toward him with the Word of God in your mouth; which is the sword of the Spirit. This is spiritual warfare! When you release that Word of God from your mouth, it will cut down the enemy. Here are few examples.

- ❖ **Has the enemy attacked your body with sickness and disease?** Advance against him declaring **Isaiah 53:5 and Psalm 103:3**!

*"Satan, I rebuke you in the Name of Jesus and I do not receive this demon of infirmity. According to Isaiah 53:5, Jesus was wounded for my transgressions and bruised for my iniquities. He was chastised for my peace and by His stripes, I am healed. Therefore, I declare that my body is whole, free of all disease and is in perfect health!"*

- ❖ **Has the enemy attacked your marriage with division and strife?** Advance against him declaring **Mark 10:8-9** and **Galatians 5: 22-23**!

*"Satan, I rebuke you in the Name of Jesus and renounce every spirit of strife and division. "According to Mark 10:8-9 & Galatians 5:22-23, God has joined this marriage together and no one can separate it. Therefore, I declare that we are one flesh, bound together by the Holy Spirit, and we manifest all the fruit of the spirit which are love, joy, peace, longsuffering, kindness, goodness, faithfulness, gentleness and self-control."*

- ❖ **Has the enemy attacked your children with rebellion?** Advance against him declaring **Psalm 127:3-5**, **Proverbs 22:6** and **Proverbs 3:5-6**!

*"Satan, I rebuke you in the Name of Jesus and I command the spirit of rebellion you have sent against my children to leave. According to Psalm 127:3-5, Proverbs 22:6, & Proverbs 3:5-6, my children are my inheritance, reward, and arrows from the Lord. I have trained them in the way of the Lord and they shall never depart from it. Therefore, I declare that my children belong to God and completely trust, obey,*

*and submit to His leadership."*

- ❖ **Has the enemy attacked your mind with confusion, depression and double-mindedness?** Advance against him declaring **1 Corinthians 14:33, Psalm 16:11,** and **Ephesians 1:17**!

*"Satan, I rebuke you in the Name of Jesus and I renounce every spirit of confusion, depression, and double-mindedness. "According to 1 Corinthians 14:33, Psalm 16:11 & Ephesians 1:17, God is a not the author of confusion, fear, or anxiety. I have the mind of Christ. Therefore, I think Godly thoughts, have peace and am never confused. I live in His presence and experience fullness of joy and pleasure daily. Therefore, I am not depressed. I have the spirit of wisdom and revelation and I always make good decisions fast. Therefore, I am not double-minded or afraid."*

- ❖ **Has the enemy attacked your finances?** Advance against him declaring **Luke 6:38, 2 Corinthians 9:10,** and **Malachi 3:10-11**!

*"Satan, I rebuke you In the Name of Jesus and I break off the spirit of poverty and lack from my life. I am an extravagant giver, a sower, a tither, a lender and not a borrower. According to Luke 6:38, 2 Corinthians 9:10, and Malachi 3:10-11, I am a tither and I have more than enough to sow and store. The Lord rebukes the devourer from my life and gives me seed to the sow and bread to eat. Therefore, I am rich and do not lack any good thing. The Lord has opened the windows of heaven over my life and poured out an abundance of blessings for me and my household."*

> *"But David said to Saul, "Your servant was tending his father's sheep. When a lion or a bear came and took a lamb from the flock, I went out after him and attacked him, and rescued it from his mouth; and* **when he rose up against me, I seized him** *by his beard and*

*struck him and killed him.* – **1 Samuel 17:34-35 (NASB) (emphasis mine)**

In David, we see the heart of a true warrior. Though he was small in stature he was not fearful in battle. In 1 Samuel 17:34-35, when a lion or bear took one of his sheep, he went and retrieved it. If the animal then turned against him after he retrieved it, he advanced toward it and kill it. He was not a bully and he did not go around "picking fights" with his enemies but if the fight came to him he would not back down. The scripture shows that he did not initially seek to kill the animals, he only advanced to kill them when they advanced toward him. We should follow the same principle.

> *"As **Goliath moved closer to attack**, David quickly ran out to meet him"* - **1 Samuel 17:48 (NLT) (emphasis mine)**

> *"Then David said to the Philistine, "You come to me with a sword, a spear, and a javelin, but I come to you in the name of the LORD of hosts, the God of the armies of Israel, whom you have taunted."* – **1 Samuel 17:45 (AMP)**

David went to the battlefield to meet Goliath. However, **Goliath initiated the fight by advancing** toward David on the battlefield. At that moment, David had to decide. He could either fight or take flight. Instead of running away from the giant, David ran quickly toward him in **the Name of the Lord**. David could boldly advance toward his enemy because he was confident in the Name of the Lord and the knowledge that God fights for His children.

> *"Now thanks be unto God, which always causeth us to triumph in Christ, and maketh manifest the savour of his knowledge by us in every place"* - **2 Corinthians 2:14 (KJV)**

# ONE MONTH WITH A KING

*"The wicked flee when no man pursueth: but the righteous are bold as a lion."* – **Proverbs 28:1 (KJV)**

David's job was simple. Be bold, advance toward the adversary in faith and trust *Yahweh-Nissi* (The LORD is my banner) (Exodus 17:15 NLT). When provoked by the enemy, you too must boldly advance against him and declare the Word of God concerning your situations. You have the Sword of the Spirit so you should use it. You are armed with the Name of The Lord who is your Banner and will cause you to always triumph. Remember, no weapon that is formed against you will prosper. Boldly advance!

❖ Now, turn to Lesson Twelve in your companion **"One Month with A King: *Interactive Study Journal"*** to complete the corresponding GEM.

## LESSON THIRTEEN

## UNCOMMON VICTORIES REQUIRE UNCOMMON TRAINING

*"Your servant has killed both the lion and the bear; and this uncircumcised Philistine will be like one of them, since he has taunted the armies of the living God."* - **I Samuel 17:36 (NASB)**

*"If it had not been the Lord who was on our side, When men rose up against us, Then they would have swallowed us alive; When their wrath was kindled against us;"* - **Psalm 124:2-3 (NKJV)**

Take a minute and reflect on a difficult battle in which The Lord gave you victory. Perhaps, you received miraculous restoration from a financial challenge, dysfunctional relationship, terminal illness, marital betrayal, relentless addiction, depression or even barrenness. It could be anything that comes to mind as long as the specific challenge you faced was extremely difficult to overcome. Remember, despite what you went through, you now have a testimony to share. Hallelujah! He brought you through it. **AMEN!**

Now, think about what The Lord did to bring you through that uncommon victory. Did He call you into an uncommon season of prayer and fasting, intimate worship, consecration or Bible study? Did He send someone with a prophetic Word to declare that you were "coming out" of that situation? Did you have to war in the Spirit and declare the Word of God daily? Leading up to that major victory, did God slowly build your faith through smaller victories? Take some time to reminisce a bit.

# ONE MONTH WITH A KING

*"We can rejoice, too, when we run into problems and trials, for we know that they help us develop endurance. And endurance develops strength of character, and character strengthens our confident hope of salvation."* - **Romans 5:3-4 (NLT)**

At your lowest point, you may have felt like it was never going to change. However, to make it through, you patiently endured the journey and, in the process, you gained strength, character, confidence and a greater hope in Christ. Whatever customized training curriculum The Lord designed for you in the midst of your trial, once completed, it led to your uncommon victory. He's a great God! Hallelujah! You can now testify that with all the lessons learned in your times of trouble, it ultimately was the power of the Living God which gave you that uncommon victory.

David's defeat of Goliath was an uncommon victory. To win an epic battle against a career warrior like Goliath required training in hand-to-hand combat, psychological warfare, and weapons. In the natural, it would be completely impossible for an unskilled civilian to defeat a decorated military general on the battlefield. This is especially true in hand-to-hand combat when the civilian has a clear height and size disadvantage.

Still, David's uncommon victory required an extended period of uncommon training. We typically think that David's foray into military engagement began when he set foot on the battlefield to face Goliath. Not so! His training began the first day his father assigned him to watch the sheep and culminated the day he snatched victory for Israel out of the jaws of defeat.

From the Psalms, we know that David spent a significant amount of time cultivating his relationship with the Lord through worship and prayer in the solitude. We know that he successfully killed at least one lion and one bear in hand-to-hand combat. We know that he understood the power of words because he prophesied to Goliath that he would kill him and behead him with his own sword. We know that David fought without fear because ran toward Goliath in the heat of battle and did not retreat.

> *Then one of the servants answered and said, "Look, I have seen a son of Jesse the Bethlehemite, who is skillful in playing, a mighty man of valor, a man of war, prudent in speech, and a handsome person; and the Lord is with him." Therefore Saul sent messengers to Jesse, and said, "Send me your son David, who is with the sheep."* - **1 Samuel 16:18-19 (NKJV)**

Something special happened in David's life during his time taking care of sheep in the wilderness. He learned new rules of engagement that differed from typical civilian life. By the time Saul's servant shared David's story, David was an anointed musician, brave leader, warrior, skillful orator and man of God. He may have entered the wilderness a recruit, but he left as a soldier of The Lord.

The United States of America has the most powerful military in the world. It's resources, impact and capabilities are unmatched globally. To build a successful military like in the US, personnel are needed to function in a variety of combat and non-combat roles. Yet, regardless of the role, nobody can serve in the US military without basic training. Today, the US Army's basic training is defined as "*the initial instruction of new military personnel. This training is a physically and psychologically intensive process, which resocializes recruits for the demands of military employment.*" (Military.com, 2018).

Over this 10-week journey, each recruit must master specific weekly tasks to progress to the next week. At the culmination of the program, recruits graduate as U.S. Army soldiers ready for battle. When David was preparing for his role in the Armies of The Living God, he also went through basic training. In fact, I've identified a few common threads between David's process and the basic training of US army recruits.

**Week Zero – Reception**: The transformation from civilian life to the Army world begins here. The soldiers bid farewell to their civilian clothes, get Army haircuts and begins the process of becoming physically fit (Military.com, 2018). For David, Reception Week may have started the day that he humbly submitted to his father, Jesse and accepted the lowly task of shepherding his father's sheep.

> *"And Samuel said to Jesse, "Are these all the children?" And he said, "There remains yet the youngest, and behold, he is tending the sheep." Then Samuel said to Jesse, "Send and bring him; for we will not sit down until he comes here."* - **1 Samuel 16:11 (NASB)**

**Week One – Fall In:**

> *Oh, how I love Your law! It is my meditation all the day. You, through Your commandments, make me wiser than my enemies; For they are ever with me. I have more understanding than all my teachers, For Your testimonies are my meditation. I understand more than the ancients, Because I keep Your precepts. I have restrained my feet from every evil way, That I may keep Your word. I have not departed from Your judgments, For You Yourself have taught me. How sweet are Your words to my taste, Sweeter than honey to my mouth! Through Your precepts I get understanding; Therefore I hate every false way. Your word is a lamp to my feet And a light to my path.* - **Psalm 119:97-105 (NKJV)**

New rules, regulations, and processes associated with being in the Army are taught in an instructional classroom setting (Military.com, 2018). For David, the rules of engagement for his journey as a soldier in God's army came from God's law. He didn't just submit to God's regulations out of sense of duty, He loved it. He engaged his heart with scripture through consistent meditation.. As a result, he went through a process of mental transformation. God's law made him wiser than his enemies, smarter than his teachers and shrewder than his elders. Through the scriptures he learned discipline, developed his character and received guidance to make the right decisions.

**Week Two – Direction:**

> *So David came to Saul and stood before him. And he loved him greatly, and he became his armorbearer. Then Saul sent to Jesse, saying, "Please let David stand before me, for he has found favor in my sight."* - **1 Samuel 16:21-22 (NKJV)**

A Drill Sergeant or mentor is assigned. This is a transition from the classroom to the field in order to test physical and mental endurance (Military.com, 2018). David learned the protocol of the palace under the tutelage of King Saul. Even though the king acted like he didn't know who David was after David killed Goliath, they knew each other quite well. It was King Saul who sent word to David's father Jesse specifically requesting David's service in his royal court. Instantly, David went from a "forgotten" shepherd to a king-in-training.

This was also King Saul's opportunity to recognize David's potential and embrace him as a mentee. Unfortunately, King Saul insecurities as a leader preventing him from being an effective mentor.

# ONE MONTH WITH A KING

## Week Three – Endurance:

> *Now David was the son of that Ephrathite of Bethlehem Judah, whose name was Jesse, and who had eight sons. And the man was old, advanced in years, in the days of Saul. The three oldest sons of Jesse had gone to follow Saul to the battle. The names of his three sons who went to the battle were Eliab the firstborn, next to him Abinadab, and the third Shammah. David was the youngest. And the three oldest followed Saul. But David occasionally went and returned from Saul to feed his father's sheep at Bethlehem.* - **1 Samuel 17:12-15 (NKJV)**

This week's activities are built around reliance on teammates, personal endurance, and physical and mental challenges associated with simulated combat scenarios (Military.com, 2018). Even after David made it to the palace, his responsibilities as a shepherd were not totally over. He occasionally went back and forth between taking care of the king and his father's sheep. That must have been a challenging time for him.

It was also a time when he had to rely on someone else to watch the sheep as he attended to his royal duties. He had to endure this process for so long that by the time it was over his father was very old. Yet, it was worth it because the challenge of juggling two important roles helped to shape his character.

## Week Four - Marksmanship:

> *So Saul clothed David with his armor, and he put a bronze helmet on his head; he also clothed him with a coat of mail. David fastened his sword to his armor and tried to walk, for he had not tested them. And David said to Saul, "I cannot walk with these, for I have not tested them." So David took them off. Then he took his staff in*

> *his hand; and he chose for himself five smooth stones from the brook, and put them in a shepherd's bag, in a pouch which he had, and his sling was in his hand. And he drew near to the Philistine.* - **1 Samuel 17:38-40 (NKJV)**

The M16A2 rifle is the standard weapon that is issued to the army recruits. During this week they participate in rigorous marksmanship courses on how to properly hold, assemble and operate the weapon, including how to breathe and shoot from multiple positions (Military.com, 2018).

For David, his weapon of choice was a sling and a stone. Prior to fighting Goliath, when Saul offered David armor and weaponry that David hadn't tested, he refused them. He then chose the one weapon he tested during his time as shepherd. It was in the wilderness that he received his marksmanship training and it was demonstrated with his accuracy in battle. It took David one stone to kill Goliath. He was so good with a sling that Goliath had no chance.

## Week Five - Trials:

> *But David said to Saul, "Your servant used to keep his father's sheep, and when a lion or a bear came and took a lamb out of the flock, I went out after it and struck it, and delivered the lamb from its mouth; and when it arose against me, I caught it by its beard, and struck and killed it. Your servant has killed both lion and bear; and this uncircumcised Philistine will be like one of them, seeing he has defied the armies of the living God." Moreover David said, "The Lord, who delivered me from the paw of the lion and from the paw of the bear, He will deliver me from the hand of this Philistine." And Saul said to David, "Go, and the Lord be with you!"* - **1 Samuel 17:34-37 (NKJV)**

# ONE MONTH WITH A KING

The Basic Rifle Marksmanship Qualification Course and the Fit to Win Obstacle Course must be successfully completed during this week (Military.com, 2018). The best way to lose a battle is to show up unprepared. Though it appeared to many that David was an untrained soldier, he sharpened his skills through extensive trials in the wilderness. Goliath may have been the first giant human being David faced but he wasn't the first giant creature.

**Week Six - Camaraderie:**

> *Then Jesse said to his son David, "Take now for your brothers an ephah of this dried grain and these ten loaves, and run to your brothers at the camp. And carry these ten cheeses to the captain of their thousand, and see how your brothers fare, and bring back news of them." Now Saul and they and all the men of Israel were in the Valley of Elah, fighting with the Philistines. So David rose early in the morning, left the sheep with a keeper, and took the things and went as Jesse had commanded him. And he came to the camp as the army was going out to the fight and shouting for the battle. For Israel and the Philistines had drawn up in battle array, army against army. And David left his supplies in the hand of the supply keeper, ran to the army, and came and greeted his brothers.* - **1 Samuel 17:17-22 (NKJV)**

Bonds are formed, and confidence is gained through trust in the platoon during the completion of trust exercises fir this week (Military.com, 2018). David's training regimen included an attempt at camaraderie. Perhaps, it was not as successful as it could have been, but it was a good gesture that eventually changed David's life. His father sent him with supplies for his brothers and their military leadership. Jesse valued his family and even though David was not always welcome with them, he was sent as an emissary to his brothers. In 1 Samuel 30, as a decorated military general,

David demonstrated what he learned about camaraderie after they defeated the Amalekites. Some of the troops who went to battle refused to share the spoils of victory with others who stayed behind and watched the supplies. Not only did David explain that both groups were equally important for their victory, it was God who gave it to them. Moreover, he made it a statute that camaraderie be demonstrated in every battle. Like the famous saying from Alexandre Dumas of The Three Musketeers; *"All for one and one for all, united we stand divided we fall."*

**Week Seven - Confidence:**

> *Then David said to the Philistine, "You come to me with a sword, with a spear, and with a javelin. But I come to you in the name of the Lord of hosts, the God of the armies of Israel, whom you have defied. This day the Lord will deliver you into my hand, and I will strike you and take your head from you. And this day I will give the carcasses of the camp of the Philistines to the birds of the air and the wild beasts of the earth, that all the earth may know that there is a God in Israel. Then all this assembly shall know that the Lord does not save with sword and spear; for the battle is the Lord's, and He will give you into our hands."*
> - **1 Samuel 17:45-47 (NKJV)**

Hand grenade training, live fire exercises, foot marching; and overall physical fitness is tested on the Confidence Course during this week (Military.com, 2018). Before David defeated Goliath, he went through his own confidence course with God. Perhaps, it took place in the wilderness while watching his father's sheep or in the palace while serving the king. What's clear is that by the time he stood before Goliath he was confident. He knew that he was going to win, and he was bold enough to declare it! Confidence in is crucial in warfare.

# ONE MONTH WITH A KING

## Week Eight - Combat Skill Development:

*Blessed be the Lord my Rock, Who trains my hands for war, And my fingers for battle -* **Psalm 144:1 (NKJV)**

Combat skills can be the difference between life and death in battle. During this week, recruits are trained in direct combat (Military.com, 2018). What recruits learn during this week will carry them through their military careers. Though David was a skilled warrior, he had no formal military training. His combat skills training came directly from God. In other words, he had a God-given ability to fight which he developed and perfected while defending his father's sheep from lions and bears.

## Week Nine - Victory Forge:

*So it was, when the Philistine arose and came and drew near to meet David, that David hurried and ran toward the army to meet the Philistine. Then David put his hand in his bag and took out a stone; and he slung it and struck the Philistine in his forehead, so that the stone sank into his forehead, and he fell on his face to the earth. So David prevailed over the Philistine with a sling and a stone, and struck the Philistine and killed him. But there was no sword in the hand of David. Therefore David ran and stood over the Philistine, took his sword and drew it out of its sheath and killed him, and cut off his head with it. And when the Philistines saw that their champion was dead, they fled. -* **1 Samuel 17:48-51 (NKJV)**

In this penultimate week of basic training recruits go on a field retreat as a final test of skills, spirit, and a demonstration of their capacity to be U.S. soldiers (Military.com, 2018). For David, Victory Forge took place on the battlefield with Goliath. It was the ultimate test of his wit, skills, courage and faith in God. While King Saul and the armies of Israel cowered in fear at the sound of Goliath's voice, David confidently approached the giant for his final test.

With five smooth stones and a sling, he knew that God had brought him through a journey of uncommon training to that very point. After the preliminary "trash-talk" was complete, David went on the offensive, running toward Goliath and launching a stone at the giant's head in the Name of the Lord. He didn't miss the target and the rest is history. With that victory, David was launched into the public eye and his journey to the throne began in earnest.

**Week Ten - Graduation:**

> *So David went out wherever Saul sent him, and behaved wisely. And Saul set him over the men of war, and he was accepted in the sight of all the people and also in the sight of Saul's servants. Now it had happened as they were coming home, when David was returning from the slaughter of the Philistine, that the women had come out of all the cities of Israel, singing and dancing, to meet King Saul, with tambourines, with joy, and with musical instruments. So the women sang as they danced, and said: "Saul has slain his thousands, And David his ten thousands."* - **1 Samuel 18:5-7 (NKJV)**

The end of basic training is the cause of great celebration. Family and friends watch their loved ones graduate and see their dreams of becoming US soldiers come true (Military.com, 2018) King Saul responded immediately to David's victory over Goliath by commissioning him as an army general. The king saw David's talent and put it to work in his favor. When David finally made it home, his fame preceded him. People came out from all around Israel to celebrate his return with dancing and singing. It was the end of training and the beginning of his new life as a soldier.

# ONE MONTH WITH A KING

*"And there shall come forth a rod out of the stem of Jesse, and a Branch shall grow out of his roots: And the spirit of the* LORD *shall rest upon him, the spirit of wisdom and understanding, the spirit of counsel and might, the spirit of knowledge and of the fear of the* LORD;*"* - **Isaiah 11:1-2 (KJV)**

Uncommon training brought about an uncommon victory for David and set into motion God's victorious plan for the coming Messiah, Jesus Christ. At any point, David could have rejected, bypassed, delayed, or deserted God's unorthodox training process but he did not. Each act of obedience, submission, prayer, worship, combat training, prophetic declaration and character testing prepared him for the challenge ahead and eventual victory. Ultimately, David's years of uncommon training conditioned his heart to love, trust, obey and rely completely on God. This same principle is true for us!

- ❖ Now, turn to Lesson Thirteen in your companion ***"One Month with A King: Interactive Study Manual"*** to complete the corresponding GEM.

## LESSON FOURTEEN

## GOD ALONE CAN CAST THE FIRST STONE

> *"Then David put his hand in his bag and took out a stone; and he slung it and struck the Philistine in his forehead, so that the stone sank into his forehead, and he fell on his face to the earth. So David prevailed over the Philistine with a sling and a stone, and struck the Philistine and killed him. But there was no sword in the hand of David."*
> **– 1 Samuel 17:49-50 (NKJV)**

Interestingly, the battle between David and Goliath appears to have been very short. When we hear the word "battle" we often imagine fierce conflict, weapons clashing, and fiery exchanges between the opposing parties. Though, in this "battle", only one stone was thrown, and it landed in Goliath's forehead.

> *Then David said to the Philistine, "You come to me with a sword, with a spear, and with a javelin. But I come to you in the name of the Lord of hosts, the God of the armies of Israel, whom you have defied. This day the Lord will deliver you into my hand, and I will strike you and take your head from you. And this day I will give the carcasses of the camp of the Philistines to the birds of the air and the wild beasts of the earth, that all the earth may know that there is a God in Israel. Then all this assembly shall know that the Lord does not save with sword and spear; for the battle is the Lord's, and He will give you into our hands."*
> **- 1 Samuel 17:45-47(NKJV)**

Though David's sling launched the first stone, God's hand propelled him to victory over Goliath. The scripture clearly emphasizes that there was no sword in David's hand.

# ONE MONTH WITH A KING

Hence, no credit for David's victory could be given to man-made tools or tactics. Just like he did against the lion and the bear, David slew the giant Goliath without any sophisticated weapons in his hand.

> *"Some trust in chariots and some in horses, but we trust in the name of the LORD our God."* - **Psalm 20:7 (NIV)**

God's track record was good with David. God had already empowered David to strike down a lion and a bear with his bare hands (1 Samuel 17:34-36). Based on those experiences, David understood that God could give him the victory with or without physical weapons of war. Therefore, David's choice of an ordinary stone and sling was not surprising (1 Samuel 17:40).

David's faith did not lie in his ordinary man-made tools but in the extraordinary name of the Lord. In his own strength, David was no match for Goliath but truly, Goliath was no match for The Lord. Remember, the Lord is your Rock and He has given you His Word to use in battle. So today, set your flesh aside, submit to His Word and let Him cast the first stone.

> *But Jesus went to the Mount of Olives. Now early in the morning He came again into the temple, and all the people came to Him; and He sat down and taught them. Then the scribes and Pharisees brought to Him a woman caught in adultery. And when they had set her in the midst, they said to Him, "Teacher, this woman was caught in adultery, in the very act. Now Moses, in the law, commanded us that such should be stoned. But what do You say?" This they said, testing Him, that they might have something of which to accuse Him. But Jesus stooped down and wrote on the ground with His finger, as though He did not hear. So when they continued asking Him, He*

*raised Himself up and said to them, "He who is without sin among you, let him throw a stone at her first." –* **John 8:1-7(NKJV)**

Are you in a battle that has been raging for a long time? Are you tired of fighting in your own strength and need God to bring it to a quick end? It's time to put down your carnal weapons of arguing, reasoning, worrying, and physical combat.

Those who live by the sword will die by the sword and those who live by the flesh will die by the flesh. When you are faced with adversity, you should not seek to fight in your own strength. Get your flesh out of the way and let God cast the first stone.

> *For though we walk in the flesh, we do not war according to the flesh. For the weapons of our warfare are not carnal but mighty in God for pulling down strongholds, casting down arguments and every high thing that exalts itself against the knowledge of God, bringing every thought into captivity to the obedience of Christ, and being ready to punish all disobedience when your obedience is fulfilled.* **- 2 Corinthians 10:3-6 (NKJV)**

David had the heart of a fighter and won many battles. Yet, David understood who and what he was fighting for. He also understood who he was fighting against. Hence, he always sought The Lord before entering any battle. He considered each battle to be a small part of a bigger spiritual war between The Lord who was on His side and God's enemies.

> *"Finally, my brethren, be strong in the Lord and in the power of His might. Put on the whole armor of God, that you may be able to stand against the [k]wiles of the devil. For we do not wrestle against flesh and blood, but*

*against principalities, against powers, against the rulers of the darkness of this age, against spiritual hosts of wickedness in the heavenly places. Therefore take up the whole armor of God, that you may be able to withstand in the evil day, and having done all, to stand. Stand therefore, having girded your waist with truth, having put on the breastplate of righteousness, and having shod your feet with the preparation of the gospel of peace; above all, taking the shield of faith with which you will be able to quench all the fiery darts of the wicked one. And take the helmet of salvation, and the sword of the Spirit, which is the word of God; praying always with all prayer and supplication in the Spirit, being watchful to this end with all perseverance and supplication for all the saints—"* – **Ephesians 6:10-18 (NKJV)**

It's time to follow David's example and fight the right way. Win the war in the spirit first so that you can enjoy supernatural victories as they manifest in the natural. Put on every piece of the armor of God (Ephesians 6:11) and wield the powerful sword of the spirit which is The Word of God (Ephesians 6:17).

*"For the word of God is living and powerful, and sharper than any two-edged sword, piercing even to the division of soul and spirit, and of joints and marrow, and is a discerner of the thoughts and intents of the heart."* – **Hebrews 4:12 (NKJV)**

*"And take the helmet of salvation, and the sword of the Spirit, which is the word of God;"* – **Ephesians 6:17 (NKJV)**

*"Is not My word like a fire?" says the Lord, "And like a hammer that breaks the rock in pieces?"* - **Jeremiah 23:29 (NKJV)**

*"That He might sanctify and cleanse her with the washing of water by the word,"* – **Ephesians 5:26 (NKJV)**

The scripture uses a host of objects to describe the Word of God, including as a type of weapon. The Word of God is quick, powerful and sharp (Hebrews 4:12). At times, the Word is called a sword (Ephesians 6:17), hammer (Jeremiah 23:29), fire, (Jeremiah 23:29), and water (Ephesians 5:26).

*"…And the Word became flesh and dwelt among us, and we beheld His glory, the glory as of the only begotten of the Father, full of grace and truth."* - **John 1:14 (NKJV)**

*"…And all drank the same spiritual drink. For they drank of that spiritual Rock that followed them, and that Rock was Christ.* – **1 Corinthians 10:4 (NKJV)**

*"Jesus said to them, "Have you never read in the Scriptures: The stone which the builders rejected has become the chief cornerstone. This was the Lord's doing, and it is marvelous in our eyes'?"* – **Matthew 21:42 (NKJV)**

Jesus is referred to as the Word made flesh (John 1:14). Jesus, the Word, is also called a rock (1 Corinthians 10:4) and a stone (Matthew 21:42). Therefore, stop wasting time fighting with carnal weapons and use your mouth to hurl the Word of God at your enemy. Speak the Word and put a stop to your enemy's advancement in the spirit!

- ❖ Now, turn to Lesson Fourteen in your companion **"One Month with A King: *Interactive Study Journal"*** to complete the corresponding GEM.

## LESSON FIFTEEN

## INVISIBLE ARMOR, INVINCIBLE GOD

*"Then Saul clothed David with his garments and put a bronze helmet on his head, and he clothed him with armor. David girded his sword over his armor and tried to walk, for he had not tested them. So, David said to Saul, "I cannot go with these, for I have not tested them." And David took them off."* – **1 Samuel 16:38-39 (NASB)**

Saul offered David armor and weapons that he had never used before, but David refused because he had not tested and couldn't trust them in battle. Those we Saul's weapons and that was Saul's armor. They fit Saul and may or may not have worked for him. The Bible didn't provide any information about Saul's military prowess using his armor and weapons, so we can only guess.

*For the weapons of our warfare are not carnal, but mighty through God to the pulling down of strong holds."* – 
**2 Corinthians 10:4 (KJV)**

David had armor which could not be seen and invisible weapons which were invincible. No, I'm not talking about his sling and stones. By themselves, they were not good enough to defeat a heavily armed military legend like Goliath. In fact, when Goliath saw the crude weapons in David's hands, he thought it was a joke. What Goliath could not see is what eventually hurt him. David had the name of The Lord and that was all he really needed to defeat Goliath.

*"By his divine power, God has given us everything we need for living a godly life. We have received all of this by coming to know him, the one who called us to himself by means of*

*his marvelous glory and excellence." -* **2 Peter 1:3 (NLT)**

Many people allow themselves to embrace the carnal wisdom of the world to fight spiritual battles. I am amazed by the number of people who trust what they see on talk shows, are easily influenced by reality tv or sift through internet blogs and psychic columns looking for advice on dealing with life's challenges. Sadly, this type of thinking is not limited to unbelievers. Sometimes, Children of God utilize these worldly tools. However, The Bible should be our "go to" for all things concerning life and godliness.

*"For the wisdom of this world is foolishness (absurdity, stupidity) before God; for it is written [in Scripture], "[He is] THE ONE WHO CATCHES THE WISE and CLEVER IN THEIR CRAFTINESS;" -* **1 Corinthians 3:19 (AMP)**

*"For the word of God is living and active and full of power [making it operative, energizing, and effective]. It is sharper than any two-edged sword, penetrating as far as the division of the soul and spirit [the completeness of a person], and of both joints and marrow [the deepest parts of our nature], exposing and judging the very thoughts and intentions of the heart." -* **Hebrews 4:12 (AMP)**

As Christians, the wisdom of this world is foolishness to us and we must REJECT it! Our mandate is to put our trust in the Word of God as our tested, tried, and true standard for victorious living. When we put on the spiritual armor of God, we are protected and able to stand against the devil and all his wicked schemes (Ephesians 6:10). Therefore, we must remember that God is our banner and in His armor we are invincible.

*"Then Saul dressed David in his garments and put a*

*bronze helmet on his head, and put a coat of mail (armor) on him. Then David fastened his sword over his armor and tried to walk, [but he could not,] because he was not used to them. And David said to Saul, "I cannot go with these, because I am not used to them." So David took them off. Then he took his [shepherd's] staff in his hand and chose for himself five smooth stones out of the stream bed, and put them in his shepherd's bag which he had, that is, in his shepherd's pouch. With his sling in his hand, he approached the Philistine. The Philistine came and approached David, with his shield-bearer in front of him. When the Philistine looked around and saw David, he derided and disparaged him because he was [just] a young man, with a ruddy complexion, and a handsome appearance. The Philistine said to David, "Am I a dog, that you come to me with [shepherd's] staffs?" And the Philistine cursed David by his gods. The Philistine also said to David, "Come to me, and I will give your flesh to the birds of the sky and the beasts of the field." Then David said to the Philistine, "You come to me with a sword, a spear, and a javelin, but I come to you in the name of the LORD of hosts, the God of the armies of Israel, whom you have taunted. This day the LORD will hand you over to me, and I will strike you down and cut off your head. And I will give the corpses of the army of the Philistines this day to the birds of the sky and the wild beasts of the earth, so that all the earth may know that there is a God in Israel, and that this entire assembly may know that the LORD does not save with the sword or with the spear; for the battle is the LORD'S and He will hand you over to us."* – **1 Samuel 16:38 – 47 (AMP)**

King Saul's gesture of offering his choice armor and helmet to David appeared to be good-natured. There's no obvious reason to question the king's intention for doing something like that for a brave, young man. Any soldier would have accepted the honor of being seen in the king's garments, helmet, and sword in battle. However, when given the opportunity to adorn them, David quickly refused them because **he had not had the opportunity to test them**.

I greatly admire David's wisdom. He chose not to go into battle with tools he was unfamiliar with. He was not accustomed to wearing visible armor and was not prepared to change what worked before. Furthermore, he had not even tested the reliability of Saul's armor. On the other hand, David was very familiar with the protection and reliability of God. David's past victories proved that he did not need man-made, fallible, visible armor because God's invisible armor was invincible.

> *"He who dwells in the shelter of the Most High will remain secure and rest in the shadow of the Almighty [whose power no enemy can withstand]. I will say of the Lord, "He is my refuge and my fortress, my God, in whom I trust [with great confidence, and on whom I rely]!"* - **Psalm 91:1-2 (AMP)**

> *The name of the Lord is a strong tower; The righteous run to it and are safe.* - **Proverbs 18:10 (NKJV)**

> *"In conclusion, be strong in the Lord [draw your strength from Him and be empowered through your union with Him] and in the power of His [boundless] might."* - **Ephesians 6:10 (AMP)**

King Saul, Goliath and their armies all marveled at David's choice to go out to battle without visible armor. It made no sense to them because they had no understanding of spiritual things. David dwelt under the shadow of the Almighty and The Lord was his refuge and fortress (Psalm 91:2). David faced Goliath with the name of the Lord (1 Samuel 17:45), which was also his invisible strong tower

(Proverbs 18:10). David's strength came from The Lord (Ephesians 6:10). God's invisible armor made David invincible. Be like David. Put on your invisible spiritual armor, use your invisible spiritual weapons. Be invincible!

- ❖ Now, turn to Lesson Fifteen in your companion **"One Month with A King: *Interactive Study Journal"*** to complete the corresponding GEM.

## LESSON SIXTEEN

## AVOID IMAGINATION EXAGGERATION

> *"This made Saul very angry. "What's this?" he said. "They credit David with ten thousands and me with only thousands. Next they'll be making him their king!"* - **1 Samuel 18:8 (NASB)**

> *"Trust in and rely confidently on the Lord with all your heart and do not rely on your own insight or understanding. In all your ways know and acknowledge and recognize Him, and He will make your paths straight and smooth [removing obstacles that block your way]."* - **Proverbs 3:5-6 (AMP)**

Have you ever heard the phrase "use your head"? It's usually meant to encourage people to apply their intellect to resolve issues or dilemmas. It is true that God has given us the ability to think and formulate creative solutions. Still, this ability can tempt us to lean on our own understanding and make decisions without consulting the Lord.

The other extreme is "analysis paralysis" which is defined as *"the condition of being unable to make a decision due to the availability of too much information which must be processed in order for the decision to be made"* (yourdictionary.com, 2018). In this instance, one becomes indecisive and is unable to move forward with a decision. Essentially, you must ensure that you are not relying on your own understanding instead of relying on Him in decision making. (Proverbs 3:5-6).

> *"For God has not given us a spirit of fear, but of power and of love and of a sound mind"* - **2 Timothy 1:7 (NKJV)**

> *"We are destroying sophisticated arguments and every exalted and proud thing that sets itself up against the [true] knowledge of God, and we are taking every thought and purpose captive to the obedience of Christ,"* - **2 Corinthians 10:5 (AMP)**

It is easy to over-think matters and get carried away with wrong imaginations leading to exaggerated conclusions. These exaggerations can cause people to make shocking decisions that are rooted in fear. The continual meditation on fearful thoughts instead of faith-filled thoughts can cause our most dreaded fears to manifest in our lives (Job 3:25). Fear is not from God, but the enemy (2 Timothy 1:7). We must be careful that we do not entertain imaginations that exalt themselves against the knowledge of God and aggressively cast them down.

> *"Then Herod, when he had secretly called the wise men, determined from them what time the star appeared. And he sent them to Bethlehem and said, "Go and search carefully for the young Child, and when you have found Him, bring back word to me, that I may come and worship Him also… Then Herod, when he saw that he was deceived by the wise men,* **was exceedingly angry; and he sent forth and put to death all the male children** *who were in Bethlehem and in all its districts, from two years old and under, according to the time which he had determined from the wise men."* – **Matthew 2:7-8 & 16 (NKJV) (emphasis mine)**

Throughout scripture, imagination exaggeration ran rampant through the minds of insecure leaders and kings. One example was King Herod. In his imagination, he greatly exaggerated the threat to his kingdom by the birth of Jesus as King of Jews. His fear and insecurity caused him to lie to the wise men so they would reveal the location of Jesus' birthplace. His motivation was to kill one child and eliminate the perceived threat to his throne. Once he realized that the wise men would not disclose his location, out of anger, Herod ordered a baby massacre.

> *"So David went out wherever Saul sent him, and he acted wisely and prospered; and Saul appointed him over the men of war. And it pleased all the people and also Saul's servants. As they were coming [home], when David returned from killing the Philistine, the women came out of all the cities of Israel, singing and dancing, to meet King Saul with tambourines, [songs of] joy, and musical instruments. The women sang as they played and danced, saying,* **"Saul has slain his thousands, and David his ten thousands. Then Saul became very angry, for this saying displeased him; and he said, "They have ascribed to David ten thousands, but to me they have ascribed [only] thousands. Now what more can he have but the kingdom?"** *Saul looked at David with suspicion [and jealousy] from that day forward. Now it came about on the next day that an evil spirit from God came forcefully on Saul, and he raved [madly] inside his house, while David was playing the harp with his hand, as usual; and there was a spear in Saul's hand. Saul hurled the spear, for he thought, "I will pin David to the wall." But David evaded him twice. Now Saul was afraid of David, because the LORD was with him, but had departed from Saul. So Saul had David removed from his presence and appointed him as his commander of a thousand; and he publicly associated with the people. David acted wisely and prospered in all his ways, and the LORD was with him. When Saul saw that he was prospering greatly, he was afraid of him. But all Israel and Judah loved David, because he publicly associated with them."* – **1 Samuel 18:5-16 (AMP) (emphasis mine)**

# ONE MONTH WITH A KING

David experienced the wrath of King Saul because the king greatly exaggerated the women's songs of joy. In Saul's imagination, the fact that the women credited David with slaying tens of thousands of soldiers in battle in contrast to his thousands was a sign that his kingdom was in jeopardy. He was not upset that the women were cheering about Israel's victories in battle. He was upset that their cheers credited David with being more victorious than he. It might sound petty to someone on the outside looking in but in Saul's mind it was a legitimate concern.

His insecurity caused him to think far beyond that moment and fear that the people would instantly want to make David king. Though David would become king in the far future, Saul's exaggerated imagination drove him to immediate fear. Thus, Saul continuously made poor choices affecting his fame, family, and fate. When he preoccupied himself with false arguments concerning David and future events, he opened the door for the enemy to influence his decision-making and subsequent actions. If Saul had done things the right way, perhaps God would have allowed the transition to David's rulership to be much smoother.

> *"For though we walk in the flesh, we do not war according to the flesh. For the weapons of our warfare are not carnal but mighty in God for pulling down strongholds, casting down arguments and every high thing that exalts itself against the knowledge of God, bringing every thought into captivity to the obedience of Christ, and being ready to punish all disobedience when your obedience is fulfilled."* -
> **2 Corinthians 10:3-6 NKJV**

Like Saul, we can easily fall into the trap of the enemy if we fail to remember that though we walk in the flesh we do not war according to the flesh. The real war takes place in the spirit and the real battleground is in our minds. Instead of feeling intimidated by the success of others, we should rejoice for what God is doing in their lives. One person's success does not diminish another person's success, nor can it stop God's purpose. Our God is great and there is enough success to go around for all of us as we remain in Him.

You can rest. There is no need for fear, competition, anxiety or insecurity. Find comfort in knowing that He is God and His unique plan for your life is not diminished when He blesses someone else. Therefore, when contrary thoughts arise, intentionally arrest them. Yank down any strongholds that the enemy seeks to erect and exalt against the knowledge of God. The arresting, pulling down, and subjecting of your thoughts to the Word of God is your responsibility, not God's. If you do not aggressively war against ungodly thoughts, they will lead to you to detrimental actions.

> *"Finally, brethren, whatever things are true, whatever things are noble, whatever things are just, whatever things are pure, whatever things are lovely, whatever things are of good report, if there is any virtue and if there is anything praiseworthy—meditate on these things. The things which you learned and received and heard and saw in me, these do, and the God of peace will be with you."* –
> **Philippians 4:8-9 (NKJV)**

Make a conscious decision today to take control of the battlefield of your mind. Choose where you want to focus your thoughts by feeding your mind with all that is good and pure. Don't leave your imagination open for the enemy to play games and destroy your life. Fill your mind with positive thoughts from The Word of God then take every negative thought captive and place them under submission to the Word of God.

❖ Now, turn to Lesson Sixteen in your companion

## ONE MONTH WITH A KING

**"One Month with A King: *Interactive Study Journal"*** to complete the corresponding GEM.

# ONE MONTH WITH A KING

# PART V

# AS FOR CHARACTER? …FLAWLESS

# ONE MONTH WITH A KING

## INTRODUCTION

> *"And endurance develops strength of character, and character strengthens our confident hope of salvation. And this hope will not lead to disappointment. For we know how dearly God loves us, because He has given us the Holy Spirit to fill our hearts with His love."* – **Romans 5:4-5 (NLT)**

**Character** is the main ingredient in fulfilling the calling that God has on our lives. The word character is defined as "*One of the attributes or features that make up and distinguish an individual; a feature used to separate distinguishable things into categories; the complex of mental and ethical traits marking and often individualizing a person, group, or nation; or moral excellence and firmness*" *(Merriam Webster Open Dictionary)*.

I have heard it said, *"Don't let your gifts take you, where your character can't keep you."* Our character must be flawless. When faced with trials and temptations, we must resist the enemy and endure, even when our flesh rages against us. This endurance will help strengthen our character and prepare us for greater victories in the future. How can we maintain a character that is flawless? Through our submission to the indwelling Holy Spirit.

In surveying the life of King David in Part V, you will discover the next four lessons and along the way, complete activities in the companion "**One Month with A King: *Interactive Study Journal*"**.

17. Be excellent in what is good
18. Be innocent of evil
19. Don't stay home during times of war
20. Retreat to the promise, not your past

## LESSON SEVENTEEN

## BE EXCELLENT IN WHAT IS GOOD

*"Then the commanders of the Philistines went out to battle, and it happened as often as they went out, that David behaved himself more wisely than all the servants of Saul. So his name was highly esteemed."* – **1 Samuel 18:30 (NASB)**

What's your reputation among your peers? Are you considered to be virtuous? Do you easily succumb to peer pressure and compromise? Believe it or not, your peers are intently scrutinizing your actions. If you profess to be a Christian, do not forget that the world is watching you. The world is looking for those who will not only preach a good message but live it out.

*"Therefore, since we are surrounded by such a huge crowd of witnesses to the life of faith, let us strip off every weight that slows us down, especially the sin that so easily trips us up. And let us run with endurance the race God has set before us."*- **Hebrews 12:1 (NLT)**

Whether justified or not, as a Christian, you will be severely criticized by many in the world when you make mistakes or fall short of God's expectations. Yet, at the same time, there are others silently cheering for you to get things right. As you demonstrate authenticity and noble character in your Christian walk, you will pique the interest of unbelievers and hopefully win some to Christ.

*"Then this Daniel, because of the extraordinary spirit within him, began distinguishing himself among the commissioners and the satraps, and the king planned to*

*appoint him over the entire realm."* - **Daniel 6:3 (AMP)**

*"For the report of your obedience has reached everyone, so that I rejoice over you, but I want you to be wise in what is good and innocent in what is evil."* - **Romans 16:19 (AMP)**

As an Ambassador of Christ you must model a spirit of excellence in what is good and remain innocent of evil among men. That is the example set by Jesus when He walked the earth and is the type of reputation that pleases The Lord. In an upside-down world that seems to value what is bad and despise what is good, people with an excellent spirit are a refreshing sight in God's eyes.

*"Pride goes before destruction, and haughtiness before a fall."* - **Proverbs 16:18 (NLT)**

*"But he gives us even more grace to stand against such evil desires. As the Scriptures say, "God opposes the proud but favors the humble."* - **James 4:6 (NLT)**

Good character includes being sensitive to the Christian walk of other believers. Though you may have victory over sin in an area, that area may still be a battleground for another believer. Bad character, on the other hand is demo, thus causing a weaker believer to stumble.

*"But you must be careful so that your freedom does not cause others with a weaker conscience to stumble. For if others see you—with your "superior knowledge"—eating in the temple of an idol, won't they be encouraged to violate their conscience by eating food that has been offered to an idol? So because of your superior knowledge, a weak believer for whom Christ died will be destroyed. And when you sin against other believers by encouraging them to do*

*something they believe is wrong, you are sinning against Christ. So if what I eat causes another believer to sin, I will never eat meat again as long as I live—for I don't want to cause another believer to stumble.* **–1 Corinthians 8:9-13 (NLT)**

Apostle Paul addressed the issues of insensitivity, selfishness and compromise in his first letter to the Corinthian church. In this letter, he also revealed his character by disclosing his resolve to embrace self-denial in order to win the lost for the sake of the gospel.

*"Even though I am a free man with no master, I have become a slave to all people to bring many to Christ. When I was with the Jews, I lived like a Jew to bring the Jews to Christ. When I was with those who follow the Jewish law, I too lived under that law. Even though I am not subject to the law, I did this so I could bring to Christ those who are under the law. When I am with the Gentiles who do not follow the Jewish law,[a] I too live apart from that law so I can bring them to Christ. But I do not ignore the law of God; I obey the law of Christ. When I am with those who are weak, I share their weakness, for I want to bring the weak to Christ. Yes, I try to find common ground with everyone, doing everything I can to save some. I do everything to spread the Good News and share in its blessings.* **– 1 Corinthians 9:19-23 (NLT)**

David modeled a spirit of excellence. Due to his defeat of Goliath, marriage to King Saul's daughter, and victories on the battlefield, David enjoyed great fame. In the eyes of the world around him, David had it all and could live however he pleased. However, David understood that with this elevated status came greater visibility and responsibility to serve God. Instead of becoming prideful in his attitude and behavior, David remained humble before God. Even when it was difficult, he continued to submit to King Saul's authority.

> *"Then you will find favor with both God and people, and you will earn a good reputation."* - **Proverbs 3:4 (NLT)**

David's name was held in high esteem (1 Samuel 18:30) among the servants of Saul because of his godly character. He stood out because he was careful with his words, actions, and had a good attitude. Regardless of the behavior of any of Saul's servants, David maintained a humble and reverent posture before God.

> *"Now it came about on the next day that an evil spirit from God came forcefully on Saul, and he raved [madly] inside his house, while David was playing the harp with his hand, as usual; and there was a spear in Saul's hand. Saul hurled the spear, for he thought, "I will pin David to the wall." But David evaded him twice. Now Saul was afraid of David, because the LORD was with him, but had departed from Saul. So Saul had David removed from his presence and appointed him as his commander of a thousand; and he publicly associated with the people. David acted wisely and prospered in all his ways, and the LORD was with him. When Saul saw that he was prospering greatly, he was afraid of him. But all Israel and Judah loved David, because he publicly associated with them."* - **1 Samuel 18:10-16 (AMP)**

David's godly character enabled him to shine. He gained the favor of God and the respect of those who were around him. May we also walk in a manner that encourages others to do likewise.

> ❖ Now, turn to Lesson Seventeen in your companion **'One Month with A King: *Interactive Study***

*Journal"* to complete the corresponding GEM.

## LESSON EIGHTEEN

## BE INNOCENT OF EVIL

*"So he said to his men, 'Far be it from me because of the Lord that I should do this thing to my lord, the Lord's anointed, to stretch out my hand against him, since he is the Lord's anointed."* – **1 Samuel 24:6 (NASB)**

What is the first thing that comes to mind when you are faced with an opportunity to criticize or rebel against your leader? Do you give thought to the consequences your decision would have on your relationship with the Lord? Too often, slanderous words, dishonor, and rebellious actions are carelessly released without any thought for the heart of the leader and more importantly, the heart of God.

*"So you, my son, be strong [constantly strengthened] and empowered in the grace that is [to be found only] in Christ Jesus. The things [the doctrine, the precepts, the admonitions, the sum of my ministry] which you have heard me teach in the presence of many witnesses, entrust [as a treasure] to reliable and faithful men who will also be capable and qualified to teach others. Take with me your share of hardship [passing through the difficulties which you are called to endure], like a good soldier of Christ Jesus."* - **2 Timothy 2:1-3 (AMP)**

Our role is not to slander, ridicule, or disrespect our leaders but to encourage, pray for and honor them. Our love for Jesus should compel us to flee from all forms of evil, especially the sin of rebellion against the leaders he has placed over our lives. Because of our love for God and our desire to honor Him, we must make it our mission to be innocent of this type of evil.

> *"For the report of your obedience has reached to all; therefore I am rejoicing over you, but I want you to be wise in what is good and innocent in what is evil"* – **Romans 16:19 (NASB)**

Our destiny is often tied to those who God has ordained to be in our lives particularly in positions of leadership. In Genesis 13, we see that Lot's blessing and prosperity hinged on his connection to his uncle Abraham. When Lot separated from Abraham, he lost his connection to the blessing God put on Abraham's life. In the same way, it is impossible for you to receive a blessing from someone you refuse to submit to. Even if the person is willing to bless you, your failure to submit to their authority will hinder the transference of the blessing from their life to yours.

> *"Bondservants, be obedient to those who are your masters according to the flesh, with fear and trembling, in sincerity of heart, as to Christ; not with eyeservice, as men-pleasers, but as bondservants of Christ, doing the will of God from the heart,"* – **Ephesians 6:5-6 (NKJV)**

Are you desiring a promotion at your workplace from your unsaved boss? Do you see it happening anytime soon or do you see it happening at all? How did your boss respond when you expressed that desire? If it wasn't good, you're not alone. All leaders are not created equal. Some are more skilled and utilize more palatable approaches to managing people than others. However, if you spend your days slandering, complaining, rebelling and speaking evil against your supervisor you only make things worse for yourself.

> *"Therefore, I exhort first of all that supplications, prayers, intercessions, and giving of thanks be made for all men, for kings and all who are in authority, that we may lead a*

*quiet and peaceable life in all godliness and reverence." –*
**1 Timothy 2:1-2 (NKJV)**

Words of dishonor and acts of rebellion create an atmosphere that can spiritually disconnect you from the blessing that would otherwise easily transfer to your life. Even if you feel justified, to turn on your leader, as time passes, your promotion will continue to be delayed. Instead, put it in the hands of God, pray for your leader, and release words of blessing. Never forget that at the end of the day, God is the one who ultimately grants promotions, not people.

Therefore, if you rebel against anyone in leadership that God has placed over you, you are rebelling against God. Simply put, there's no way to win a war like that. Remember, God expects you to submit to your leaders and **pray for them**. If that is how God views leadership and promotion in the world, how much more within the Body of Christ.

Today, there are many church congregations that have been fractured by envy, strife, and divisions among members because of carnal reasoning and rebellion against leadership. Ironically, Apostle Paul experienced and addressed those same ungodly behaviors in his first and second letters to the Corinthian church.

> *"And I, brethren, could not speak to you as to spiritual people but as to carnal, as to babes in Christ. I fed you with milk and not with solid food; for until now you were not able to receive it, and even now you are still not able; for you are still carnal. For where there are envy, strife, and divisions among you, are you not carnal and behaving like mere men? For when one says, "I am of Paul," and another, "I am of Apollos," are you not carnal? Who then is Paul, and who is Apollos, but ministers through whom you believed, as the Lord gave to each one? I planted,*

*Apollos watered, but God gave the increase. So then neither he who plants is anything, nor he who waters, but God who gives the increase. Now he who plants and he who waters are one, and each one will receive his own reward according to his own labor. For we are God's fellow workers; you are God's field, you are God's building."* – **1 Corinthians 3:1-9 (NKJV)**

In his first letter to the Corinthians, Apostle Paul addressed the envy, strife, and divisions that were reported to him from the household of Chloe. Before Paul left Corinth, he trained and assigned Apollos as the overseer of the newly formed church.

In his absence, members from within the church separated themselves into two groups by identifying themselves as followers of either Paul or Apollos. Paul promptly addressed this carnal reasoning as evidence of their lack of maturity as believers. He reminded them that God's chosen ministers are only servants who sow the word and water what is planted. God alone brings any increase.

If God places a leader in position in a church, the growth of the people of that church is not solely contingent on the leader's ability or style. The leader's job is only to sow the seeds of God's Word into the hearts of the members, cover them in prayer, model God's love and set a high standard of spiritual maturity. At the same time, church members must receive with humility the spiritual seeds being sown into their lives. It is then God's job to produce the fruit.

*"For such are false apostles, deceitful workers, transforming themselves into apostles of Christ. And no wonder! For Satan himself transforms himself into an angel of light. Therefore it is no great thing if his ministers also transform themselves into ministers of righteousness, whose end will be according to their works."* – **2**

# ONE MONTH WITH A KING

## Corinthians 11:13-15 (NKJV)

*"Are they ministers of Christ?—I speak as a fool—I am more: in labors more abundant, in stripes above measure, in prisons more frequently, in deaths often. From the Jews five times I received forty stripes minus one. Three times I was beaten with rods; once I was stoned; three times I was shipwrecked; a night and a day I have been in the deep; in journeys often, in perils of waters, in perils of robbers, in perils of my own countrymen, in perils of the Gentiles, in perils in the city, in perils in the wilderness, in perils in the sea, in perils among false brethren; in weariness and toil, in sleeplessness often, in hunger and thirst, in fastings often, in cold and nakedness— besides the other things, what comes upon me daily: my deep concern for all the churches. Who is weak, and I am not weak? Who is made to stumble, and I do not burn with indignation? If I must boast, I will boast in the things which concern my infirmity. The God and Father of our Lord Jesus Christ, who is blessed forever, knows that I am not lying."* - **2 Corinthians 11:23-31 (NKJV)**

In his second letter to the Corinthian church, Apostle Paul addressed the false apostles who infiltrated their church. He exposed the influence of these deceitful workers as a spiritual assault against his apostleship and the Gospel of Jesus Christ. He then affirmed his love for the church and appealed to them to obey Christ instead of the doctrines presented by these false apostles masquerading as "angels of light".

Furthermore, Paul brought their credibility into question by providing accounts of his hardships, persecutions, and near-death experiences as a truly appointed apostle of Christ. In contrast, these false apostles simply boasted of their own accomplishments without any valid experiences to substantiate their claims as apostles. Now fast forward to our time. Many Christians despise true apostles who serve daily in their local churches and flock toward charismatic false teachers or flashy media personalities whose goal is not to edify but to deceive.

> *"He said to his men, "The LORD forbid that I should do this thing to my master, the LORD'S anointed, to put out my hand against him, since he is the anointed of the LORD." -* **1 Samuel 24:6 (AMP)**

David loved God and lived a life of reverence for his anointed leader, Saul. Though Saul was determined to kill him, David never sought to retaliate because it would grieve the heart of God. David was given multiple occasions to retaliate against Saul, yet he did not. David reverently understood that to harm God's anointed servant Saul would be an act of war against God.

Even when it seemed hard, David chose to be innocent of evil by surrendering to God's divinely appointed leadership. David understood that God is the one who appoints leaders and grants them authority. He entrusted his life and welfare to God knowing that God would vindicate him in due season. Read this Biblical account of David's restraint when given the opportunity to harm King Saul, God's anointed leader.

> *"When Saul returned from following the Philistines, he was told, "Behold, David is in the Wilderness of Engedi." Then Saul took three thousand chosen men out of all Israel and went to search for David and his men in front of the Rocks of the Wild Goats. On the way he came to the sheepfolds where there was a cave; and Saul went in to [relieve himself. Now David and his men were sitting in the cave's innermost recesses. David's men said to him, "Behold, this is the day of which the LORD said to you, 'Behold, I will hand over your enemy to you, and you shall do to him as seems good to you.'" Then David arose [in*

*the darkness] and stealthily cut off the hem (edge) of Saul's robe. Afterward, David's conscience bothered him because he had cut off the hem of Saul's robe. He said to his men, "The LORD forbid that I should do this thing to my master, the LORD'S anointed, to put out my hand against him, since he is the anointed of the LORD." So David strongly rebuked his men with these words and did not let them rise up against Saul. Saul got up, left the cave and went on his way.*

*Then David also got up afterward and went out of the cave and called after Saul, saying, "My lord the king!" And when Saul looked behind him, David bowed with his face to the ground and lay himself face down. David said to Saul, 'Why do you listen to the words of men who say, 'David seeks to harm you?' Behold, your eyes have seen today how the LORD had given you into my hand in the cave. Some told me to kill you, but I spared you; I said, 'I will not reach out my hand against my lord, for he is the LORD'S anointed.' Look, my father! Indeed, see the hem of your robe in my hand! Since I cut off the hem of your robe and did not kill you, know and understand [without question] that there is no evil or treason in my hands. I have not sinned against you, though you are lying in wait to take my life. May the LORD judge between me and you; and may the LORD avenge me on you; but my hand shall not be against you. As the proverb of the ancients says, 'Out of the wicked comes wickedness'; but my hand shall not be against you. After whom has the king of Israel come out? Whom do you pursue [with three thousand men]? A dead dog, a single flea? May the LORD be the judge and render judgment between me and you; and may He see and plead my cause and vindicate me by saving me from your hand."*

*When David had finished saying these words to Saul, Saul said, "Is this your voice, my son David?" Then Saul raised*

> *his voice and wept. He said to David, "You are more righteous and upright [in God's eyes] than I; for you have done good to me, but I have done evil to you. You have declared today the good that you have done to me, for when the LORD put me into your hand, you did not kill me. For if a man finds his enemy, will he let him go away unharmed? So may the LORD reward you with good in return for what you have done for me this day. Now, behold, I know that you will certainly be king and that the kingdom of Israel will be established in your hand. So now swear to me by the LORD that you will not cut off my descendants after me and that you will not destroy my name from my father's household (extended family)." David gave Saul his oath; and Saul went home, but David and his men went up to the mountain stronghold."* - **1 Samuel 24:1-22 (AMP)**

Like David, we must be innocent of evil by submitting to the men and women God has established as leaders over our lives. Whether they are our parents, supervisors, pastors, or government officials, God has granted them authority.

Are you adhering to the leadership structure the Lord has placed over your life? Are there evil attitudes or behaviors that you need to change or avoid? Take some time to reflect today. Reinforce what is right and adjust what is wrong so that you will be innocent of evil.

> *"Everyone must submit to governing authorities. For all authority comes from God, and those in positions of authority have been placed there by God"* - **Romans 13:1 (NLT)**

> *"Obey them that have the rule over you, and submit yourselves: for they watch for your souls, as they that must give account, that they may do it with joy, and not with grief: for that is unprofitable for you"* - **Hebrews 13:17**

# ONE MONTH WITH A KING

## (KJV)

❖ Now, turn to Lesson Eighteen in your companion **"One Month with A King: *Interactive Study Journal"*** to complete the corresponding GEM.

## LESSON NINETEEN

## DON'T STAY HOME DURING TIMES OF WAR

> *"Then it happened in the spring, at the time when kings go out to battle... David stayed at Jerusalem."* - **2 Samuel 11:1 (NASB)**

Why did David stay in Jerusalem? What happened as a result of his decision? Before we tackle those questions let's establish some core truths. God has a perfect plan for our lives. To access this perfect plan, we must be in the right place at the right time. First, we must remember to trust Him. Second, we must believe that His timing is perfect. All in all, He has promised to direct our paths if we trust Him and acknowledge Him in every aspect of our lives.

> *"Trust in the LORD with all thine heart; and lean not unto thine own understanding. In all thy ways acknowledge him, and he shall direct thy paths."* – **Proverbs 3:5-6 (KJV)**

> *"To everything there is a season, and a time to every purpose under the heaven"* - **Ecclesiastes 3:1 (KJV)**

Whether we are in times of war or times of peace, the best place to be is in the Will of God. It is imperative that we consistently obey the Voice of The Lord so that we will be properly positioned for divine appointments only He can orchestrate. As His children, we do not have the luxury of picking and choosing which occasions we wish to obey His Voice. Our very life depends on the daily promptings of Holy Spirit.

At all times and in every season, we must be rightly

positioned in order to experience all that God has ordained for us. With each failure to obey His voice, we run the risk of making decisions which can negatively impact our lives and the lives of countless others around us.

We have all heard stories or personally experienced these supernatural instances when we have been in the right place at the right time. Also, we have all heard stories of individuals who forfeited their destinies or even died because they were in the wrong place at the wrong time, the right place at the wrong time or the wrong place at the right time.

For instance, kids who skip school and end up in trouble, workers who don't show up to work consistently or on time and lose their jobs or Christians who abandon their post in the local church and face difficult times. Whatever it is, nothing good comes out of being out of position. It is our responsibility to ensure that we are in the right position at the right time so that we avoid life-long negative consequences and successfully reach our God-ordained destinies.

David learned this lesson the hard way. During the spring, when kings go out to battle, he chose to stay in Jerusalem. Unfortunately, he was not in the right place for that this season of his life. As the Commander-in-Chief, he failed to pray and seek the Lord before making the decision to remain home during a time of war. That single choice set in motion a series of events that changed the trajectory of his personal future.

> *"One evening David got up from his couch and was walking on the [flat] roof of the king's palace, and from there he saw a woman bathing; and she was very beautiful in appearance."* –
> **2 Samuel 11:2 (AMP)**

## ONE MONTH WITH A KING

Since David was not rightly positioned at war, he opened himself up to his true enemy, the devil. Due to his newfound free time, he ended up wrongly positioned on the roof where he saw Bathsheba bathing and the rest is literally history. He committed adultery with her resulting in her pregnancy then tried to cover it up by calling her husband, Uriah, home from the battlefield. After that plan didn't work, he sent Uriah back to the war with the following orders.

> *"He wrote in the letter, "Put Uriah in the front line of the heaviest fighting and leave him, so that he may be struck down and die."* – **2 Samuel 11:15 (AMP)**

What started as a simple decision to stay home from war turned into the worst decision of David's life. Because he was out of place, David's lust became the catalyst for a chain reaction of adultery, impregnation, and murder. After Uriah died, The Lord sent the Prophet Nathan to convict David of his sin and prophesy the consequences.

> *"Why have you despised the commandment of the Lord, to do evil in His sight? You have killed Uriah the Hittite with the sword; you have taken his wife to be your wife, and have killed him with the sword of the people of Ammon. Now therefore, the sword shall never depart from your house, because you have despised Me, and have taken the wife of Uriah the Hittite to be your wife.' Thus says the Lord: 'Behold, I will raise up adversity against you from your own house; and I will take your wives before your eyes and give them to your neighbor, and he shall lie with your wives in the sight of this sun. For you did it secretly, but I will do this thing before all Israel, before the sun.' So David said to Nathan, "I have sinned against the Lord." And Nathan said to David, "The Lord also has put away your sin; you shall not die. However, because by this deed you have given great occasion to the enemies of*

# ONE MONTH WITH A KING

*the Lord to blaspheme, the child also who is born to you shall surely die."* – **2 Samuel 12:9-15 (NKJV)**

David's wrong decision did more than affect his own life, it negatively impacted the lives of Bathsheba (2 Samuel 11:2), Uriah (2 Samuel 11:15), the child (2 Samuel 12:15) and the members of David's entire family. Though he repented of his sin, his family continued to reap the consequences for a generation.

There are so many valuable lessons to be learned from David's experience. The Lord faithfully orders your steps so that you can ultimately reach your destiny. Along the journey, He opens supernatural doors, creates vital connections, and orchestrates perfectly ordained moments that are necessary for your development. Take responsibility today for your actions and ensure that you are in the right position at the right time to enjoy what God has for you.

Whenever you are supposed to be at work, do not fabricate excuses to stay home. When you are supposed to be at school, do not skip class to run the streets with your friends. When you are supposed to be home sleeping in your own bed, do not spend the night sleeping in someone else's bed. When you are supposed to be on the computer researching, do not surf and view pornography. When you are supposed to be at church interceding with the prayer warriors, don't stay home during times of war. Remember, one decision can change your life forever. Therefore, pray and ask Holy Spirit to help you make the right one.

- ❖ Now, turn to Lesson Nineteen in your companion **"One Month with A King: *Interactive Study Journal"*** to complete the corresponding GEM.

## LESSON TWENTY

## RETREAT TO THE PROMISE, NOT YOUR PAST

> *"Now David fled and escaped and came to Samuel at Ramah, and told him all that Saul had done to him. And he and Samuel went and stayed in Naioth."* - **1 Samuel 19:18 (NASB)**

Where do you go when your reality seems completely opposite to the prophetic words you received from God? What do you do when your perfectly formulated life plans appear to be spinning out of control? What direction do you choose when there seems to be darkness all around?

You retreat! Yes, that's right... RETREAT! However, do not retreat to your past acquaintances or old lifestyle but retreat and return to the promises that God has spoken over your life.

> *"For no matter, how many promises God has made, they are "Yes" in Christ. And so through him the "Amen" is spoken by us to the glory of God"* - **2 Corinthians 1:20 (NIV)**

In times of doubt, there are two steps you must take. First, you must remember the promises God has given you in His Word. Then, you must recall all the prophetic words He has declared over your life. If God has made a promise to you concerning your spouse, children, education, career, health, or destiny, He will keep it.

> *"God is not a man, so he does not lie. He is not human, so he does not change his mind. Has he ever spoken and failed to act? Has he ever promised and not carried it*

*through."* - **Numbers 23:19 (NLT)**

*"And the LORD will make you the head and not the tail; you shall be above only, and not be beneath, if you heed the commandments of the LORD your God, which I command you today, and are careful to observe them"* - **Deuteronomy 28:13 (NKJV)**

Unlike human beings, God does not make rash or emotional vows. He is also never pressured or manipulated into making promises. He can fulfill any promises He has ever made concerning your life. Whenever natural circumstances appear different from God's promises, do not despair. Instead, return to the truths that God has spoken about your future and destiny.

The Lord has spoken many prophetic words over my life. Many of which I have already seen come to pass, while others are yet to manifest. I would love to say that every day I am on cloud-9 while waiting for these promises. To be completely honest, there are moments when it seems hard to see that the promises are just over the horizon.

However, instead of losing hope and retreating in defeat I choose to retreat to the promises of God. I encourage myself in the Lord by worshipping God for who He is and thanking Him for what He has promised to do. I also remind myself of His promises by reading and reflecting on the written prophetic words I have received from Him.

I declare scriptures that align with these prophetic promises to silence the voice of the enemy. I also play all my prophetic words that have been recorded on CDs and tapes. *Yes, I said "tapes".* Bottom line, I retreat to the promises of God.

*"Now Eliab his oldest brother heard what he said to the men; and Eliab's anger burned against David and he said, "Why have you come down here? With whom did you leave those few sheep in the wilderness? I know your presumption (overconfidence) and the evil of your heart; for you have come down in order to see the battle."* - **1 Samuel 17:28 (AMP)**

*"Then Samuel said to Jesse, "Are all your sons here?" Jesse replied, "There is still one left, the youngest; he is tending the sheep." Samuel said to Jesse, "Send word and bring him; because we will not sit down [to eat the sacrificial meal] until he comes here."* - **1 Samuel 16:11 (AMP)**

When David fled from King Saul, the first place he ran to was to his spiritual father, the Prophet Samuel (1 Sam. 19:18). Samuel was the one who originally heard from God and anointed David as the chosen king of Israel. It is interesting that he did not return home to his older brothers or his earthly father, Jesse. His older brothers never supported him, and one accused him of being conceited and wicked-hearted (1 Samuel 17:28). On the other hand, his earthly father only saw him as a shepherd (1 Samuel 16:11). Not as a potential king.

*"Then Samuel took the horn of oil and anointed David in the presence of his brothers; and the Spirit of the LORD came mightily upon David from that day forward. And Samuel arose and went to Ramah."* - **1 Samuel 16:13 (AMP)**

*"Remember the word to Your servant, In which You have made me hope."* – **Psalm 119:49 (NASB)**

The fact that David chose to retreat to Samuel's house

shows that he felt he would be safe, affirmed, and encouraged there. David knew that Samuel would speak life into him and remind him of who God declared him to be at his anointing ceremony (1 Samuel 16:13). He would help him recall his anointing ceremony and the reality that he is God's chosen king. As the prophet who anointed David to be king, Samuel represented God's promises which provided David with the reassurance he needed.

So, what do you do when you are in trouble? Where do you run when things seem to be falling apart around you? Run to the Word of God. Retreat to God's promises and be encouraged. Remember the Word that God has spoken over your life and maintain your hope in Him.

- ❖ Now, turn to Lesson Twenty in your companion **"One Month with A King: *Interactive Study Journal"*** to complete the corresponding GEM.

# PART VI
# LEAD TO SERVE

# ONE MONTH WITH A KING

## INTRODUCTION

*"But he who is greatest among you shall be your servant. And whoever exalts himself will be humbled, and he who humbles himself will be exalted."* – **Matthew 23:11-12 (NKJV)**

Leadership is defined *as "the act or an instance of leading people" (Merriam Webster Open Dictionary)*. My personal philosophy is that leadership is about serving people. In order to lead people, you must see the best in them and desire the best for them. In the Kingdom of God, leadership is defined by servanthood. We are the most like Jesus when we lay down our lives in service to those that He has entrusted to us.

We must serve well, knowing that we will give an account to God for the way we cared for those He placed under our influence. These relationships may come in the form of our children, spouses, employees, mentees, peers, church members, or authorities.

In surveying the life of King David in Part VI, you will discover the next four lessons and along the way, complete activities in the companion **"One Month with A King: *Interactive Study Journal"*.**

21. God is in the shepherding business
22. The Lord will send you apprentices – *Embrace them!*
23. The Lord will send you allies – *Recognize them!*
24. Sow a leader - Reap an army

# ONE MONTH WITH A KING

## LESSON TWENTY-ONE

## GOD IS IN THE SHEPHERDING BUSINESS

*"David was the youngest son. David's three oldest brothers stayed with Saul's army, but David went back and forth so he could help his father with the sheep in Bethlehem."* - **1 Samuel 17:14-15 (NLT)**

You've probably heard that sheep are not the brightest members of God's animal kingdom, nor are they the cleanest. They are also known to be very high maintenance and defenseless against their predators. The scientific name for domesticated sheep is *Ovis aries*. Adult male sheep are also known as rams, while the females are called ewes.

Ewes give birth to baby sheep which are affectionately known as lambs. Sheep are prey species whose only defense is fleeing danger. Since domestic sheep are not intelligent, they require the care of a shepherd in order to survive. Without a shepherd to protect, feed, and shear them, domestic sheep will quickly die.

As human beings, we are intelligent and considered God's highest creation. The scripture says that we were created only a little lower than Elohim (Psalms 8:5). Yet, we do not always make intelligent decisions, are prone to filthiness and require a lot of maintenance. The truth is, without the blood of Jesus, we would be completely defenseless against the attacks of Satan (Revelation 12:22).

*"I am the good shepherd. The good shepherd gives His life for the sheep."* - **John 10:11(NKJV)**

*My sheep hear my voice, and I know them, and they follow*

> *me"* - **John 10:27 (NKJV)**

> *"The Lord is my shepherd; I shall not want. He makes me to lie down in green pastures; He leads me beside the still waters."* – **Psalm 23:1-2 (NKJV)**

> *"Know that the Lord, He is God; It is He who has made us, and not we ourselves; We are His people and the sheep of His pasture."* - **Psalm 100:3 (NKJV)**

It is no wonder that God refers to us as sheep and Himself as the Good Shepherd. Jesus is our provider, peace, and leader. Shepherding is a dirty business filled with mundane tasks, unpleasant circumstances, and danger. To be successful, the shepherd has to truly love the sheep and lay down his life in service to them. Jesus is Jehovah Rohi and He passionately loves us!

> *"Your servant has killed both lion and bear; and this uncircumcised Philistine will be like one of them, seeing he has defied the armies of the living God."* - **1 Samuel 17:36 (NKJV)**

> *"David was the youngest son. David's three oldest brothers stayed with Saul's army, but David went back and forth so he could help his father with the sheep in Bethlehem."* – **1 Samuel 17:14-15 (NKJV)**

David was in the shepherding business, before becoming king over Israel. He faithfully fed, washed, and protected his father's sheep against a lion and a bear. Even after David was given his first role within Saul's army, he faithfully maintained his shepherding responsibilities in Bethlehem. David's new-found role in Saul's army could have served as a perfect excuse to rid himself of his shepherding job, but he did not neglect it.

*"Your servant has killed both lion and bear; and this uncircumcised Philistine will be like one of them, seeing he has defied the armies of the living God."* - **John 3:16 (NKJV)**

*"And I will pray the Father, and He will give you another Helper, that He may abide with you forever"* - **John 14:16 (NKJV)**

Jesus is in the shepherding business! He is the Good Shepherd who demonstrated His love for us by dying on the Cross as the Lamb. After His death and resurrection, He then sent us a Helper who continues to guide us (John 3:16, John 10:11, & John 14:16). Despite our poor decisions, filthiness, complaining, and weakness, Jesus still does not neglect His shepherding responsibilities. Daily, He feeds us with His Word, washes us with His blood and protects us by the power of the Holy Spirit. He has never neglected His sheep nor ever will He.

Even today, if a sheep goes astray, He leaves the other ninety-nine and fiercely goes after them. He does not want a single sheep to perish. Jesus is saving lives everyday and we can partner with Him by diligently sharing the Gospel through evangelism!

*"If a man has a hundred sheep and one of them wanders away, what will he do? Won't he leave the ninety-nine others on the hills and go out to search for the one that is lost? And if he finds it, I tell you the truth, he will rejoice over it more than over the ninety-nine that didn't wander away! In the same way, it is not my heavenly Father's will that even one of these little ones should perish."* – **Matthew 18:12-14 (NLT)**

*"So let's not get tired of doing what is good. At just the right time we will reap a harvest of blessing if we don't give up."* - **Galatians 6:9 (NLT)**

We all have tasks that we may not enjoy doing. Sometimes, those tasks include good things that God ordained for us to do. May we develop stronger character, so we can stick with our responsibilities even when they seem mundane and unpleasant. We cannot grow weary in doing what is right. The Lord is watching our daily decisions and activities to see if we will be faithful in tasks small and great. He will reward our faithfulness and we will reap a blessing if we don't faint.

❖ Now, turn to Lesson Twenty-One in your companion **"One Month with A King: *Interactive Study Journal"*** to complete the corresponding GEM.

## LESSON TWENTY-TWO

## GOD WILL SEND YOU APPRENTICES – EMBRACE THEM

*"Everyone who was in distress, and everyone who was in debt, and everyone who was discontented gathered to him; and he became captain over them. Now there were about four hundred men with him."* – **1 Samuel 22:2 (NASB)**

The Lord is a good Father. *"Every good gift and every perfect gift is from above, and cometh down from the Father of lights, with whom is no variableness, neither shadow of turning"* (James 1:17 KJV). He equips and trains up His children to fulfill the destinies He has for them. As a part of our development, He may grant us the privilege of serving as mentors to others.

*"Similarly, teach the older women to live in a way that honors God. They must not slander others or be heavy drinkers. Instead, they should teach others what is good. These older women must train the younger women to love their husbands and their children, to live wisely and be pure, to work in their homes, to do good, and to be submissive to their husbands. Then they will not bring shame on the word of God."* - **Titus 2:3-5 (NLT)**

Whether it is due to wisdom, age, or experience, opportunities to mentor others are God-ordained and precious in the sight of God. When they come, we are to embrace them because they are signs that God trusts us to impart something eternal into the lives of others.

David was a gift to King Saul just as much as King Saul was a gift to David. Through Saul, David gained an understanding of palace affairs, kingdom protocol, and the rules of warfare. Through David, Saul was given the opportunity to duplicate his knowledge, share his leadership expertise, and grow in character. Unfortunately, Saul viewed David as a threat rather than a gifted mentee. Too often, leaders become intimated by their subordinates who are talented and demonstrate the potential for success. Instead of nurturing, grooming and providing support, they seek to undermine their growth. Why not focus on securing the future of the mission?

As leaders, mentorship should be considered an opportunity as opposed to a threat. Instead of being intimidated by the people coming up behind you embrace them and mentor them to success. Mentorship affords benefits not only to the mentee by also the mentor. While mentees get the opportunity to learn, grow and develop into leaders, mentors receive the benefits of loyalty, duplicating themselves, sharpening their knowledge, and the privilege of helping someone become better.

> *"So David left Gath and escaped to the cave of Adullam. Soon his brothers and all his other relatives joined him there. Then others began coming—men who were in trouble or in debt or who were just discontented—until David was the captain of about 400 men. Later David went to Mizpeh in Moab, where he asked the king, "Please allow my father and mother to live here with you until I know what God is going to do for me." So David's parents stayed in Moab with the king during the entire time David was living in his stronghold. One day the prophet Gad told David, "Leave the stronghold and return to the land of Judah." So David went to the forest of Hereth.* - **1 Samuel 22:1-5 (NKJV)**

Ironically, while David was fleeing from Saul, the Lord sent a band of men to him for mentorship. God sent men who were distressed, in debt and discontented. At that time, they really had nothing to offer. This seemed to be the least likely time for David to be able to impart to anyone because he, himself was in great need. Still, instead of rejecting these men, David embraced them and trusted in the Lord for wisdom to impart to them. As a result of his investment, he reaped the benefits of loyalty, duplicating himself, sharpening his own knowledge and helping them all become better.

By mentoring others, David became better prepared for his kingship. He drew on his experiences in the wilderness, war, and worship. Through mentoring, David duplicated his characteristics and transform four hundred downtrodden men (1 Samuel 22:2) into a loyal army who did mighty exploits. Let's look at a few of the characteristics David instilled in the lives of his mentees.

**Leadership**:
*"These are the names of the mighty men whom David had: Josheb-Basshebeth the Tachmonite, chief among [b]the captains..."* - **2 Samuel 23:8 (NKJV)**

*"Now Abishai the brother of Joab, the son of Zeruiah, was chief of [a]another three...he became their captain"* - **2 Samuel 23:18-19 (NKJV)**

*"...Benaiah the son of Jehoiada...David appointed him over his guard..."* - **2 Samuel 23:22-23 (NKJV)**

**Valor:**
*"Josheb-Basshebeth the Tachmonite...He was called Adino the Eznite, because he had killed eight hundred men at one time."* - **2 Samuel 23:8 (NKJV)**

*"Eleazar the son of [a]Dodo, the Ahohite, ... defied the*

*Philistines who were gathered there for battle, and the men of Israel had retreated. He arose and attacked the Philistines until his hand was weary, and his hand stuck to the sword."* - **2 Samuel 23:9-10 (NKJV)**

*"...Shammah the son of Agee the Hararite. The Philistines had gathered together into a troop ...But he stationed himself in the middle of the field, defended it, and killed the Philistines."* - **2 Samuel 23:9-10 (NKJV)**

*"Abishai son of Zeruiah, the brother of Joab, ... once used his spear to kill 300 enemy warriors in a single battle."* - **2 Samuel 23:18 (NLT)**

*"...Benaiah son of Jehoiada, a valiant warrior[a] from Kabzeel. He did many heroic deeds, which included killing two champions[b] of Moab... Another time, on a snowy day, he chased a lion down into a pit and killed it. ...Once, armed only with a club, he killed an imposing Egyptian warrior who was armed with a spear. Benaiah wrenched the spear from the Egyptian's hand and killed him with it."* - **2 Samuel 23:20-21 (NLT)**

## Service:

*"And David said..."Oh, that someone would give me a drink of the water from the well of Bethlehem, ... the three mighty men broke through the camp of the Philistines, drew water from the well of Bethlehem...and took it and brought it to David.-* **2 Samuel 23:15-16 (NLT)**

## Character:

*"...and Uriah the Hittite: thirty-seven in all."* -***2 Samuel 11:11 (NKJV)***

*"And Uriah said...and my lord Joab and the servants of my lord are encamped in the open fields. Shall I then go to my house...to lie with my wife? As you live, and as your*

# ONE MONTH WITH A KING

*soul lives, I will not do this thing."* - **2 Samuel 23:38**

### Worship:
*"Then David danced before the Lord with all his might; and David was wearing a linen ephod. So* ***David and all the house of Israel*** *brought up the ark of the Lord with shouting and with the sound of the trumpet."* - ***2 Samuel 6:14-15 (NKJV)***

God in His infinite wisdom may entrust you with the gift of someone to mentor that will be mutually beneficial. It is an opportunity for you to develop as a leader while helping someone else grow in the process. Today, look around at who the Lord has placed in your life for you to mentor. Pour into them, embrace them and watch them grow.

- ❖ Now, turn to Lesson Twenty-Two in your companion ***"One Month with A King: Interactive Study Journal"*** to complete the corresponding GEM.

## LESSON TWENTY-THREE

## GOD WILL SEND YOU ALLIES – RECOGNIZE THEM

> *"Then three of the thirty chief men went down and came to David in the harvest time to the cave of Adullam, while the troop of the Philistines was camping in the valley of Rephaim."* - **2 Samuel 23:13 (NASB)**

The road to your destiny will be filled with twists and turns and even seasons of loneliness. The good news is that even when you feel alone, you are never alone. God is always with you and will never leave you nor forsake you (Deuteronomy 31:6). He will also send you allies to aid and/or encourage you along the way to your destiny.

God is infinite in wisdom. His ways and thoughts are higher than ours. The allies He sends our way may appear in unexpected people in unusual places. These allies may come in the form of a supervisor at work, a student at school, a stranger in a taxi, a neighbor in the grocery store, an old friend overseas, or a random person walking down the street.

> *"That same day two of Jesus' followers were walking to ... Emmaus, ... Jesus himself suddenly came and began walking with them. But God kept them from recognizing him. They said to each other, "Didn't our hearts burn within us as he talked with us on the road"* - **Luke 24:13-32 (NLT)**

You never know when God will send an ally in your direction. Failure to recognize these allies can short-circuit your progress to your destiny. The presence of allies is vital because they will come to provide you with advice, opportunities, resources, and/or connections. Your ability to recognize them as gifts that the Lord has sent to aid you on your journey is imperative to you getting there. Though you may not always recognize them with your eyes, the Holy Spirit will speak and confirm their appointment in your heart.

> *"Then Joshua secretly sent out two spies from the Israelite camp ... "Scout out the land on the other side of the Jordan River, ... Jericho. So the two men ... came to the house of a prostitute named Rahab and stayed there that night...hidden...beneath bundles of flax ...Now swear to me by the LORD that you will be kind to me and my family since I have helped you"* - **Joshua 2:1-12 (NLT)**

When Joshua assigned two spies the task of scouting out the land of Jericho, The Lord appointed a prostitute by the name of Rahab as an unlikely ally. She was instrumental in hiding them from the guards of the city and providing them with a safe route to escape. In exchange for her kind allegiance, her life and the lives of her entire family were spared when the city was conquered by Israel's army (Joshua 2:1-12).

> *"Saul also sent messengers to David's house to watch him and to kill him in the morning. And Michal, David's wife, told him, saying, "If you do not save your life tonight, tomorrow you will be killed." So Michal let David down through a window. And he went and fled and escaped."* - **1 Samuel 19:11-12 (NKJV**)

> *"Now Saul spoke to Jonathan his son and to all his servants, that they should kill David; but Jonathan, Saul's son, delighted greatly in David. So Jonathan told David, saying, "My father Saul seeks to kill you. Therefore please be on your guard until morning, and stay in a secret place*

*and hide."* - **1 Samuel 19:1-2 (NKJV)**

While David fled from Saul, the Lord sent allies to assist him. Instead of allowing his pride to cause him to reject their assistance, he humbly recognized them and accepted their aid. From the palace, the Lord used his wife Michal (1 Samuel 19:20) and brother-in-law Jonathan (1 Samuel 20:1) to aid him in escaping from his father-in-law.

> *"So David fled and escaped, and went to Samuel at Ramah, and told him all that Saul had done to him. And he and Samuel went and stayed in Naioth."* - **1 Samuel 19:18 (NKJV)**

> *"Then three of the thirty chief men went down at harvest time and came to David at the cave of Adullam. And the troop of Philistines encamped in the Valley of Rephaim."* - **2 Samuel 23:13 (NKJV)**

God also allowed the Prophet Samuel (1 Samuel 19:18), a band of priests (1 Samuel 21:1), and even his enemies, the Philistines (1 Samuel 27:1) to aid David outside of the palace. Then, God sent thirty men as allies to David while he was hiding in the cave of Adullam (2 Samuel 23:13).

> *"Now to Him who is able to do exceedingly abundantly above all that we ask or think, according to the power that works in us, to Him be glory in the church by Christ Jesus to all generations, forever and ever. Amen."* – **Ephesians 3:20-21 (NKJV)**

Throughout his journey to kingship, David wisely recognized all the allies that God sent and accepted their aid. The plan that God has for your life is grander than anything you could ever think or imagine (Ephesians 3:20). The Lord has ordained specific people who can partner with you along the way. It is important to recognize these allies God may send to you and accept their assistance. Otherwise, if you try to go it alone, you may never reach your destiny.

❖ Now, turn to Lesson Twenty-Three in your companion **"One Month with A King: *Interactive Study Journal"*** to complete the corresponding GEM.

## LESSON TWENTY-FOUR

## SOW A LEADER, REAP AN ARMY

*"These are the names of the mighty men whom David had: Josheb-basshebeth,... Eleazar,... Shammah,...three of the thirty chief men..."* - **2 Samuel 23:8-13 (NASB)**

As leaders, it is important to understand that the people who work with you and work for you will not be with you forever. They are going to leave you one day. Whether it's due to promotion, relocation, retirement, or some other reason, they will not be under your leadership forever.

Leadership is a privilege and should be viewed as such. It is an opportunity to influence and positively impact the lives of others and make them better. For a short window of time, you have the unique privilege of using your influence to pull greatness out of those you lead. In return, they will serve you better and add value wherever they go after they leave you.

If your focus is solely on obtaining power, position or self-aggrandizement, then you are probably a "selfish" leader. If your focus is on equipping, empowering, and elevating others, you are probably a "self-less" leader.

In the Kingdom of God, leadership is defined by servanthood. Servant leaders employ a self-less approach to leading others. They view their leadership position as a privileged opportunity to serve and make others better. We are the most like Jesus when we lay down our lives in service to those that He has entrusted to us.

Are you a servant leader? A servant leader is characterized by one having an innate desire to first serve then lead with the motivation of meeting the needs of those around them (Greenleaf, 1970). Those who adopt this leadership style are highly effective. They have a servant's heart and lead by modeling how to meet the needs of others through sacrifice. These leaders lay down their lives in service for their followers.

> *Jesus said "I tell you the truth, unless a kernel of wheat is planted in the soil and dies, it remains alone. But its death will produce many new kernels--a plentiful harvest of new lives"* - **John 12:24 (NLT)**

> *"The Spirit of the Lord God is upon Me, because the Lord has anointed Me to preach good tidings to the poor; He has sent Me to heal the brokenhearted, to proclaim liberty to the captives, and the opening of the prison to those who are bound; to proclaim the acceptable year of the Lord, and the day of vengeance of our God; to comfort all who mourn, to console those who mourn in Zion, to give them beauty for ashes, the oil of joy for mourning, the garment of praise for the spirit of heaviness; that they may be called trees of righteousness, the planting of the Lord, that He may be glorified."* – **Isaiah 61:1-23 (NKJV)**

Jesus' entire ministry on earth was an act of service to His Father. By laying down His life He also served all of mankind. He epitomized servant leadership when He washed His disciples' feet (John 13:4), healed the sick, raised the dead, and cast out demons to set people free (Isaiah 61:1-3). His ultimate act of servant leadership was His brutal death on the cross to save us all (John 3:16).

> *"So the three mighty men broke through the camp of the*

> *Philistines, and drew water from the well of Bethlehem which was by the gate, and took it and brought it to David. Nevertheless he would not drink it but poured it out to the LORD; and he said, "Be it far from me, O LORD, that I should do this. Shall I drink the blood of the men who went in jeopardy of their lives."* - **2 Samuel 23:16-17 (NASB)**

David utilized a servant leadership approach at various times in his life. He demonstrated servant leadership by risking his life to protect his father's sheep (1 Samuel 17:36). Later, he mentored and trained distressed, depressed, and debt-ridden men while he fled from King Saul (1 Samuel 22:2). By sowing his own life in service to others, David reaped an army of world-renowned mighty men (2 Samuel 23). The men in David's army grew so loyal to him that they were willing to risk their lives breaking through the enemy's camp just to bring him a cup of water from the well of Bethlehem.

> *"But to all who believed him and accepted him, he gave the right to become children of God."*- **John 1:12 (NLT)**

> *"Greater love has no one than this, than to lay down one's life for his friends."* - **John 15:13 (NKJV)**

> *"And when he had found him, he brought him to Antioch. So it was that for a whole year they assembled with the church and taught a great many people. And the disciples were first called Christians in Antioch."* - **Acts 11:26 (NKJV)**

Love is an action, not just a feeling. Jesus' great love for us compelled him to serve by selflessly laying down His life. Yet, Jesus did not come out of the deal empty-handed. He sowed His life (John 15:13) and reaped an army of Christians (Acts 11:26). If you wish to reap an army of souls for the Kingdom of God, sow yourself in service by sharing the Gospel and modeling the love of Jesus before others.

- ❖ Now, turn to Lesson Twenty-Four in your companion **"One Month with A King: *Interactive Study Journal"*** to complete the corresponding GEM.

# ONE MONTH WITH A KING

# PART VII
# REPENT RAPIDLY

# ONE MONTH WITH A KING

## INTRODUCTION

*"Or do you think lightly of the riches of His kindness and tolerance and patience, not knowing that the kindness of God leads you to repentance?"* – **Romans 2:4 (NASB)**

Along the way to fulfilling your destiny, areas of weakness may become apparent. It is impossible to walk perfectly before the Lord apart from the power of the Holy Spirit. Hidden sin that resides in your heart may manifest resulting in you missing the mark. When this happens, the enemy will try to come and bring condemnation. This condemnation can cause you to walk under a cloud of shame and depression. The Holy Ghost is not like that.

Instead, when you do wrong, the Holy Spirit convicts you of your sin. In response, you don't need to run away from God. The conviction of the Holy Ghost is really an invitation to immediate repentance and restoration. Your response should be to fall to your knees and receive God's forgiveness. His kindness draws you to repentance and He is faithful and just to forgive you the very moment we you repent.

In surveying the life of King David in Part VII, you will discover the next three lessons and along the way, complete activities in the companion **"One Month with A King:** *Interactive Study Journal"*.

25. God keeps His covenants – even when we don't
26. Repent immediately
27. Repentance clears the sin, but not its consequences

## LESSON TWENTY-FIVE

## GOD KEEPS HIS CONVENANT EVEN WHEN WE DON'T

> *"He said to me, 'Your son Solomon is the one who shall build My house and My courts; for I have chosen him to be a son to Me, and I will be a father to him."* - **1 Chronicles 28:6 (NASB)**

What comes to mind with you hear the word covenant? Do you think of something that is sacred and holy? Do you think of something that is casual and informal? Have your experiences surrounding covenants been ones of joy and laughter or mourning and tears? A convenant is defined as a formal, solemn, and binding agreement, a written agreement or promise usually under seal between two or more parties especially for the performance of some action *(Merriam Webster Open Dictionary)*.

A covenant is different from a contract. A contract is legally binding while a covenant is a spiritual agreement. Covenants are sealed while contracts are signed. In a contractual agreement, there are mutually beneficial terms including an exit clause, while covenants are designed to be faithfully fulfilled with no way out.

> *"I will confirm my covenant with you and your descendants after you, from generation to generation. This is the everlasting covenant: I will always be your God and the God of your descendants after you"* - **Genesis 17:7 (NLT)**

As human beings, we often struggle with upholding contractual agreements and can downright fail at keeping covenants. However, God's faithfulness to us is exceedingly greater than our unfaithfulness to Him. He is a good God who always keeps His covenant. Even when we fail Him, He does not cast us away. Throughout the ages, God has proven His faithfulness.

Whatever God has promised concerning your life He will also do. We must be like Abraham who was *"... fully convinced that God is able to do whatever he promises"* (Romans 4:21 NLT). *"God is not a man, so he does not lie. He is not human, so he does not change his mind. Has he ever spoken and failed to act? Has he ever promised and not carried it through?"* (Numbers 23:19 NLT). Oh, that we would remain true to Him to the same degree that He remains true to us.

> *"Your house and your kingdom shall endure before Me forever; your throne shall be established forever"* - **2 Samuel 7:16 (NASB)**

> *"And there shall come forth a rod out of the stem of Jesse, and a Branch shall grow out of his roots"* - **Isaiah 11:1 (KJV)**

> *"And Jesse begot David the king. David the king begot Solomon by her who had been the wife of Uriah… and Jacob begot Joseph the husband of Mary, of whom was born Jesus who is called Christ"* - **Matthew 1:6-16 (NKJV)**

The Lord made an eternal promise to David concerning the establishment of his throne. Though David sinned, God did not renege on the covenant he had made. Bathsheba and David bore another son and named him Solomon (2 Samuel 12:25).

The Lord made Solomon the wisest king who ever lived (1 Kings 4:30-31) and allowed him to build God's temple instead of his father. Through this act, God kept his promise to David that, *"Your son Solomon will build my Temple and its courtyards..."* (1 Chronicles 28:6 NLT).

Most importantly, God kept his covenant with David through Jesus, the King of Kings and Lord of Lords. David's throne will continue forever because Jesus, who came to earth through the lineage of David will reign on it for eternity.

- ❖ Now, turn to Lesson Twenty-Five in your companion **"One Month with A King: *Interactive Study Journal"*** to complete the corresponding GEM.

## LESSON TWENTY-SIX

## REPENT IMMEDIATELY

*"Then David said to Nathan, "I have sinned against the Lord." And Nathan said to David, "The Lord also has taken away your sin; you shall not die." -* **2 Samuel 12:13 (NASB)**

*"For all have sinned, and come short of the glory of God;"* - **Romans 3:23 (KJV)**

We thank God for the blood of Jesus because it washes away our sin. *"He is the atoning sacrifice for our sins, and not only for ours but also for the sins of the whole world"* (1 John 2:2 NIV). To benefit from His atoning sacrifice, we must confess our sins and receive His forgiveness just like He promised.

*"If we confess our sins, he is faithful and just to forgive us our sins, and to cleanse us from all unrighteousness"* - **1 John 1:9 (KJV)**

*"There is therefore now no condemnation to them which are in Christ Jesus, who walk not after the flesh, but after the Spirit"* - **Romans 8:1 (KJV)**

Thanks be to God that if we confess our sins, He forgives us and cleanses us from all unrighteousness. In Him, there is no condemnation for our past sins. Hence, we can boldly move forward without a guilty conscience.

*"Come now, and let us reason together," Says the LORD, "Though your sins are as scarlet, They will be as white as snow; Though they are red like crimson, They will be like wool.* - **Isaiah 1:18 (NASB)**

When we delay repentance, we live under a cloud of guilt and condemnation. It is impossible for a sincere Christian to carry out a normal life with a guilty conscience. A guilty conscience causes a Christian to avoid God's presence just like Adam and Eve in the Garden of Eden (Genesis 3:8). That's not good because our fellowship with the Holy Spirit is vital to our spiritual walk. We cannot be victorious apart from Him (John 6:63). Therefore, the faster we repent the quicker the blood of Jesus can wash away our sins and clear our conscience.

> *"So the Philistines fought, and Israel was defeated, and every man fled to his tent. There was a very great slaughter, and there fell of Israel thirty thousand foot soldiers."* – **1 Samuel 4:10 (NKJV)**

In 1 Samuel 4:10, the Ark of God represented the presence of God. Whenever Israel lived righteously, the presence of God was with them and they won their battles. Whenever they sinned, the presence of God departed. In one instance, they lost a battle against the Philistines and 30,000 men were slayed.

Wherever there is "unrepented" sin, your heart drifts further and further from the presence of God. He is holy and cannot dwell in any place where there is sin. That's why quick repentance according to 1 John 1:9 is so important. The departure of the presence of the Holy Spirit is be devastating.

I heard Apostle Guillermo Maldonado describe God's presence as *"The person of God revealed in a specific matter; atmosphere and environment; and person"* When we are in His presence, we experience rest (Matthew 11:28), fullness of joy (Psalm 16:11), and fullness of peace (Jerimiah 33:6). His presence also awakens our consciousness of God, stirs up the fear of God, and causes our hearts to worship. We can practice His presence through prayer, worship, and declaration of the Word of God. However, when we fail to humble ourselves and repent, we stifle the full benefit of these experiences.

> *"So David said to Nathan, "I have sinned against the LORD." And Nathan said to David, "The LORD also has put away your sin; you shall not die"* - **2 Samuel 12:13 (NKJV)**

Though David's sin was great, His love for God was far greater. When The Lord sent the Prophet Nathan to confront David about his adultery with Bathsheba and murder of Uriah, he quickly repented.

> *"Create in me a clean heart, O God; and renew a right spirit within me. Cast me not away from thy presence; and take not thy holy spirit from me. Restore unto me the joy of thy salvation; and uphold me with thy free spirit"* - **Psalm 51: 10-12 (KJV)**

David's swift repentance provides us with the model that pleases the heart of God. David truly was a man after God's own heart (Acts 13:22). He even went on to compose Psalm 51 providing greater insight into his repentant heart. His words give us a clear illustration of a heart of deep regret for his sin.

The Lord would say to you today, don't delay. Repent of your offense, be cleansed and move forward. If you don't think you need to repent, ask The Lord to search your heart today and reveal any unconfessed sin. If there is anything there, then repent and receive His forgiveness and restoration. To God be the glory!

❖ Now, turn to Lesson Twenty-Six in your companion **"One Month with A King:** *Interactive Study Journal"* to complete the corresponding GEM.

## LESSON TWENTY-SEVEN

## REPENTANCE CLEARS THE SIN, BUT NOT ITS CONSEQUENCES

> *"However, because by this deed you have given occasion to the enemies of the Lord to blaspheme, the child also that is born to you shall surely die."* - **2 Samuel 12:14 (NASB)**

Thank God for his forgiveness and atoning sacrifice. Jesus has made a way for our sin to be removed far from us. *"As far as the east is from the west, so far hath he removed our transgressions from us."* (Psalms 103:12 KJV)

> *"He will turn again, he will have compassion upon us; he will subdue our iniquities; and thou wilt cast all their sins into the depths of the sea"* - **Micah 7:19 (KJV)**

According to Newton's Third Law of Motion, for every action, there is an equal and opposite reaction. This basically means that for every interaction, there is a pair of forces acting on the two interacting objects. Nothing that we do occurs in a vacuum and thus has a consequence. Though our repented sins are forgotten by Jesus, that doesn't eliminate all the consequences.

> *"If any of you lack wisdom, let him ask of God, that giveth to all men liberally, and upbraideth not; and it shall be given him"* - **James 1:5 (KJV)**

Many times, the effects of sin continue to play out in our lives and the lives of others for an extended period. If sexual sin results in pregnancy, someone still must raise the child. If physical sin results in someone's death, there remains the finality of loss. Whether decisions are good or bad there are always consequences. Consequently, it is important for us to ask God for His wisdom to live daily before Him.

> *"So David said to Nathan, "I have sinned against the LORD." And Nathan said to David, "The LORD also has put away your sin; you shall not die"* - **2 Samuel 12:13 (NKJV)**

> *"I gave you your master's house and your masters wives into your keeping, and gave you the house of Israel and Judah…Why have you despised the commandment of the LORD, to do evil in His sight? You have killed Uriah the Hittite with the sword; you have taken his wife to be your wife, and have killed him with the sword of the people of Ammon. Now therefore, the sword shall never depart from your house, because you have despised Me, …' Thus says the LORD: 'Behold, I will raise up adversity against you from your own house; and I will take your wives before your eyes and give them to your neighbor, and he shall lie with your wives in the sight of this sun…However, because by this deed you have given great occasion to the enemies of the LORD to blaspheme, the child also … shall surely die"* - **2 Samuel 12:8-14 (NKJV)**

David quickly repented of his sins to God. The Lord immediately washed his sins away from him. However, the effects of the sin gave the enemy an opportunity to blaspheme the Lord. The natural and spiritual consequences of David's choices were costly to him and his entire household. Some of these consequences included the death of his first child, the rape of his daughter Tamar by his son Ammon, the rebellion and murder of his son Absalom, and betrayal by his leadership team.

> *"And David's heart condemned him after he had numbered the people. So David said to the Lord, "I have*

> *sinned greatly in what I have done; but now, I pray, O Lord, take away the iniquity of Your servant, for I have done very foolishly. "Now when David arose in the morning, the word of the Lord came to the prophet Gad, David's seer, saying, "Go and tell David, 'Thus says the Lord: "I offer you three things; choose one of them for yourself, that I may do it to you." ' " So Gad came to David and told him; and he said to him, "Shall seven years of famine come to you in your land? Or shall you flee three months before your enemies, while they pursue you? Or shall there be three days' plague in your land? Now consider and see what answer I should take back to Him who sent me." And David said to Gad, "I am in great distress. Please let us fall into the hand of the Lord, for His mercies are great; but do not let me fall into the hand of man." So the Lord sent a plague upon Israel from the morning till the appointed time. From Dan to Beersheba seventy thousand men of the people died.*
> *"* – **2 Samuel 24:10-15 (NKJV)**

Later in David's life, pride caused him to take a census of Israel and Judah. However, when his heart condemned him, he repented. In response, God sent the prophet Gad to David with three options for facing the consequences of his actions. Though He repented for his sin, the consequences remained. Yet, God mercifully allowed David to choose his preferred consequence. David chose a plague that killed 70,000 Israelites.

> *"Now the Philistines fought against Israel; and the men of Israel fled from before the Philistines and fell slain on Mount Gilboa. Then the Philistines followed hard after Saul and his sons. And the Philistines killed Jonathan, Aminadab, and Malchishua, Saul's sons. The battle became fierce against Saul. The archers hit him, and he was severely wounded by the archers. Then Saul said to his armorbearer, "Draw your sword, and thrust me through*

*with it, lest these uncircumcised men come and thrust me through and [k]abuse me." But his armorbearer would not, for he was greatly afraid. Therefore Saul took a sword and fell on it. And when his armorbearer saw that Saul was dead, he also fell on his sword, and died with him. So Saul, his three sons, his armorbearer, and all his men died together that same day."* – **1 Samuel 31:1-6 (NKJV)**

King Saul also repented after giving a series of excuses for his disobedience to God. However, he still faced consequences which included losing his sons, his kingdom, and eventually his life.

> *"Do not be deceived, God is not mocked; for whatever a man sows, this he will also reap"* - **Galatians 6:7 (NASB)**

Remember, God is a great King and He will not be mocked. We will reap the consequences of each decision we make. Commit today to make the right decisions.

- ❖ Now, turn to Lesson Twenty-Seven in your companion **"One Month with A King: *Interactive Study Journal"*** to complete the corresponding GEM.

# ONE MONTH WITH A KING

# PART VIII

# WORSHIP WHOLEHEARTEDLY

# ONE MONTH WITH A KING

## INTRODUCTION

*"I will bless the Lord at all times: His praise shall continually be in my mouth. My soul shall make her boast in the Lord: the humble shall hear thereof, and be glad. O magnify the Lord with me, and let us exalt His name together. I sought the Lord, and He heard me, and delivered me from all my fears."* – **Psalm 34:1-4 (KJV)**

In every season, the Lord is worthy of praise. While you are in the wilderness awaiting the fulfillment of God's promises, your heart should remain in a posture of worship. When you are in the palace of prosperity enjoying the best life could offer, your heart should remain in the same posture of worship. Regardless of the season you are in, God is the same yesterday, today, and forever. Therefore, He is always worthy of your wholehearted honor, praise and worship, no matter the cost.

In surveying the life of King David in Part VIII, you will discover the final four lessons and along the way, complete activities in the companion **"One Month with A King: *Interactive Study Journal"*.**

28. Private worship precedes public worship
29. Only give God costly gifts
30. Worship God in the wilderness
31. Worship God in the palace

## LESSON TWENTY-EIGHT

## PRIVATE WORSHIP PRECEDES PUBLIC WORSHIP

*"So it came about whenever the evil spirit from God came to Saul, David would take the harp and play it with his hand; and Saul would be refreshed and be well, and the evil spirit would depart from him."* - **1 Samuel 16:23 (NASB)**

As Christians, the desire to spend significant time in the presence of the Lord should come naturally. The truth is that for some of us, it can be very difficult to find the time. However, the presence of the Holy Spirit living within us fiercely longs for fellowship and communion. This is found in times of worship, whether public or private. Though powerful and encouraging, public assemblies and corporate worship gatherings should not be the only places that we express our love to God.

A lifestyle of private worship must be established in the life of every born-again Christian. It is in these times of personal prayer, praise, and consecration that we develop the backbone for a pure walk with Him. These intimate moments in His presence prepare us to live surrendered lives in public and enable us to minister, serve and shift the atmosphere around us.

Smith Wigglesworth, John G. Lake, Kathryn Kuhlman, and many of God's Generals (Liardon, 1996) led lives of private worship including periods of extensive prayer and fasting. Their intimate relationships with the Holy Spirit fueled their public worship, enabling them to minister with power and authority.

David's lifestyle of private worship was the foundation for his public worship before God and man. We each must have a secret history with God. A private history of worship is not something that can be taught, transferred, or fabricated. That history is developed over time through surrendering before the throne of God. Even on days when your flesh would rather sleep longer or skip being in the presence of God altogether you still need to spend time with God.

> *"And whenever the tormenting spirit from God troubled Saul, David would play the harp. Then Saul would feel better, and the tormenting spirit would go away"* - **1 Samuel 16:23 (NLT)**

Many of David's Psalms were composed during his wilderness seasons. In Psalm 144:1, David blessed the Lord because He trains our hands for war and our fingers to battle. Why was Saul refreshed and made well whenever David played the harp? David was a true worshipper. John 4:24 (NKJV) reminds us that, *"God is Spirit, and those who worship Him must worship in spirit and truth."*

As a true worshipper, David had the spiritual authority to create an atmosphere that ushered in the Spirit of God. When the Spirit of the Lord descends on a place miracle will happen. Those who are sick receive healing, the dead are raised, and the blind receive their sight.

God illustrated this to me using the effects of a magnet hovering over shavings of steel. When the magnet is placed close to the steel shaving, in unison, they all stand at attention. As the magnet is moved to the left, all the steel shavings lean left. As the magnet is moved to the right, all the steel shavings lean right. The steel shavings are defenseless against the force of the magnet.

In the same way, the scripture says in 1 Corinthians 3:17 (NIV); *"Where the spirit of the Lord is there is liberty."* Therefore, anything or anyone that enters God's presence is "magnetized" by his power. Whatever is wrong is made right. Where this sadness, He brings joy. Where there is bondage, He brings liberty. That's the power of God's presence.

We know that David lived a life that was characterized by worship both in the pasture (Psalm 63:1-2) and the palace (1 Samuel 16:23 & 2 Samuel 6:14). David's private worship enabled his heart to remain focused on God (Acts 13:22). David's lifestyle cultivated an atmosphere for God's presence (Psalm 22:3).

Declare today, *"Jesus, You are my audience of one and I will worship you whether seen or unseen by man."*

- ❖ Now, turn to Lesson Twenty-Eight in your companion **"One Month with A King: Interactive Study Journal"** to complete the corresponding GEM.

## LESSON TWENTY-NINE

## ONLY GIVE GOD COSTLY GIFTS

> *"However, the king said to Araunah, "No, but I will surely buy it from you for a price, for I will not offer burnt offerings to the Lord my God which cost me nothing." So David bought the threshing floor and the oxen for fifty shekels of silver."*- **2 Samuel 24:24 (NASB)**

God does not require us to bring Him expensive gifts, but He does appreciate sacrificial gifts. He is not moved by our expensive jewelry, riches or anything else we could bring to Him. He is not impressed by material things because He owns everything.

> *"For all the animals of the forest are mine, and I own the cattle on a thousand hills"* - **Psalm 50:10 (NLT)**

> *"All the wood in Lebanon's forests and all Lebanon's animals would not be enough to make a burnt offering worthy of our God"* - **Isaiah 40:16 (NLT)**

God requires us to bring gifts that are costly to us as individuals. Costly is defined as *"commanding a high price especially because of intrinsic worth; made or done at heavy expense or sacrifice" (Merriam Webster Open Dictionary)*. A costly gift may be expensive, but an expensive gift may not necessarily be costly. It all depends on the person.

> *"And He looked up and saw the rich putting their gifts into the treasury, and He saw also a certain poor widow putting in two mites. So He said, "Truly I say to you that this poor widow has put in more than all; for all these out of their abundance have put in offerings for God, but she*

*out of her poverty put in all the livelihood that she had."* –
**Luke 21:1-4 (NKJV)**

Though He does not need anything materially from us, He is worthy of far more than anything we could ever offer Him. However, His heart is moved when we sacrifice and give what is personally costly to us. A prime example is the Biblical account of the woman with the mite. Jesus was moved by the cost of her gift because where she was financially at the time. It was a sacrifice for her because she had nothing left over.

> *"Then, six days before the Passover, Jesus came to Bethany, where Lazarus was who had been dead, whom He had raised from the dead. There they made Him a supper; and Martha served, but Lazarus was one of those who sat at the table with Him. Then Mary took a pound of very costly oil of spikenard, anointed the feet of Jesus, and wiped His feet with her hair. And the house was filled with the fragrance of the oil. But one of His disciples, Judas Iscariot, Simon's son, who would betray Him, said, "Why was this fragrant oil not sold for three hundred denarii and given to the poor?" This he said, not that he cared for the poor, but because he was a thief, and had the money box; and he used to take what was put in it. But Jesus said, "Let her alone; she has kept this for the day of My burial. For the poor you have with you always, but Me you do not have always.""* – **John 12:1-8 (NKJV)**

When Jesus was anointed at Bethany, He received the most expensive gift Mary could offer. Sacrificially, she anointed Jesus by emptying her costly spikenard and wiped His feet with her hair. Despite the opinions of others who were present, she persisted in her worship. Her sacrificial gift demonstrated that she would rather be materialistically bankrupt than fail to worship God wholeheartedly.

In the same way, David understood that God's heart was moved by gifts that were sacrificial. He declared *"I will not offer burnt offerings to the Lord my God which cost me nothing"* (2 Samuel 24:24, NASB). Instead of giving an offering to God that did not cost him anything, he insisted on paying fifty shekels of silver for the threshing floor and the oxen. Then, he dedicated it to God after purchasing it.

Giving is not about the amount of finances, it's about the heart of the giver. Whether it's time, service, praise, or finances, God's only requirement is that your gifts are personally sacrificial. Perhaps, you feel like you have nothing of substantial value to give God. You may have been through so much pain, disappointment, or abuse that you feel there is nothing left to give Him. On the contrary, even what you perceive as only a "mite" left over after everything you have been through is priceless in the sight of God. Your surrender of the fragments of your broken heart is of more value to God than all the gifts a person could give.

> *"I beseech you therefore, brethren, by the mercies of God, that you present your bodies a living sacrifice, holy, acceptable to God, which is your reasonable service"* – **Romans: 12:1(NKJV)**

> *"But what does it say? "The word is near you, in your mouth and in your heart" (that is, the word of faith which we preach): that if you confess with your mouth the Lord Jesus and believe in your heart that God has raised Him from the dead, you will be saved. For with the heart one believes unto righteousness, and with the mouth confession is made unto salvation.* – **Romans: 10:8-10(NKJV)**

When I reflect on the gift of salvation, mercy, forgiveness, peace of mind, protection, provision, and the countless blessings that Jesus has bestowed on my life, my heart loves Him even more. I have surrendered everything I am and all that I have to Him for His honor and glory. Today, as a demonstration of your gratitude and love for the Father, why don't you give Him the most costly gift you can give; your entire life.

❖ Now, turn to Lesson Twenty-Nine in your companion **"One Month with A King: *Interactive Study Journal"*** to complete the corresponding GEM.

## LESSON THIRTY

## WORSHIP GOD IN THE WILDERNESS

> *"David stayed in the wilderness in the strongholds, and remained in the hill country in the wilderness .... And Saul sought him every day, but God did not deliver him into his hand"* - **1 Samuel 23:14 (NASB)**

It is easy to worship God when you are in a season of prosperity. Yet, the challenge comes when the season shifts and suddenly there is a need, lack, or loss. Welcome to your wilderness season. A wilderness is defined as *"a tract or region uncultivated and uninhabited by human beings; an empty or pathless area or region"* (Merriam Webster Open Dictionary).

In the wilderness, you will experience testing, battling, and loneliness. Still, depending on your response, it can become a time of strengthening, fortification and growth. How will you respond to your wilderness season? Will you complain, mope, and focus on your negative circumstances or will you choose to worship and sing praises to God despite the challenges?

> *"Then Jesus, being filled with the Holy Spirit, returned from the Jordan and was led by the Spirit into the wilderness, being tempted for forty days by the devil. And in those days He ate nothing, and afterward, when they had ended, He was hungry."* – **Luke 4:1-2 (NKJV)**

> *"The next day John saw Jesus coming toward him, and said, "Behold! The Lamb of God who takes away the sin of the world!"* – **John 1:29 (NKJV)**

Jesus was led into the wilderness by the Holy Spirit. For

Him, the wilderness was a place where He was tested on every front by the enemy. In response to each test, He stood on the Word of God and worshipped His Heavenly Father with His obedience. The wilderness season served as an opportunity for strengthening for the next level of ministry. We know this because immedaely after Jesus emerged victoriously from the wilderness, His public ministry began.

On January 26, 2014, in obedience to the voice of God, we held our first service of The Body Church. We began meeting on Sundays in a hotel meeting room in Midtown Atlanta, GA. We felt like the children of Israel in the wilderness. Each week, we loaded our cars with speakers, cords, and boxes. It was hard work, but the joy of the Lord was our strength. We continued to pray and worship faithfully each week, regardless of how we felt, who was with us, or where we were.

Less than two years later, The Lord opened a door for us to rent a more comfortable meeting space in an office park in Decatur, GA. We were thankful for the freedom to set up our "tent" in one place and have it remain in place throughout the week.

We have seen growth and spiritual fruit in the lives of the members who have chosen to remain faithful. Though we have not yet reached the promised land that God promised, we remain thankful. It is our privilege to worship Him wholeheartedly, regardless of how we feel, who is there with us, or where we are.

We remain steadfast in prayer, worship, and the Word of God. We may not have large facilities, flashing lights, or a large worship band at the time that I am writing this book, but God is faithful. What we do have is the presence of the Holy Spirit and we will worship God, even in the wilderness.

> *"About midnight Paul and Silas were praying and singing hymns to God… Suddenly there was such a violent earthquake … prison doors flew open,"* - **Acts 16:25-26 (NIV)**

Do you remember Paul and Silas' response to imprisonment? They knew that the only way out of that difficult situation was to bring God into it. They chose to sing, worship, and let the name of the Most High God echo throughout the corridors of the prison. Their melodious sound wasn't only heard by all the prisoners but reached the very ears of Almighty God. In that dark wilderness, the light of God broke in with a miracle of freedom, as well as salvation for their captor.

> *"David stayed in the wilderness in the strongholds, and remained in the hill country in the wilderness…. And Saul sought him every day, but God did not deliver him into his hand"* - **1 Samuel 23:14 (NASB)**

> *"Because thy lovingkindness is better than life, my lips shall praise thee. Thus will I bless thee while I live: I will lift up my hands in thy name"* - **Psalm 63:3-4 (KJV)**

For David, the wilderness seasons of his life never changed his worship. Instead, he consistently worshipped God and was delivered from his enemies. During solitary days as a shepherd, he gained a revelation of the goodness of God and composed songs unto the Lord.

> *"The LORD is my shepherd; I have all that I need."* - **Psalm 23:1 (NLT)**

While fleeing from King Saul, David was protected by the Lord and remembered His goodness and mercy. Even after he became king, David continued to sing of God's lovingkindness in the wilderness as he fled from his own son, Prince Absalom.

> *"Thou preparest a table before me in the presence of mine enemies: ... Surely goodness and mercy shall follow me all the days of my life..."* - **Psalm 23:5-6 (KJV)**

David worshipfully declared that God's goodness and mercy were in pursuit of him instead of his enemies. God delivered him from his enemies as he chose to worship, even in the wilderness.

When you look back over your life, how have you responded to God when you were in the wilderness? The children of Israel murmured in their wilderness season, ultimately prolonging the season and forfeiting their entrance into the Promised Land. Instead of worshipping God, they re-considered their commitment and reverted to their old customs and idolatry.

Wilderness seasons are seasons when your faith is tested, and perseverance is produced (James 1:2-3). So, make the best of it. I have heard it said that when life gives you lemons, make lemonade and sell it. Stay focused on the goodness of God and keep worshipping Him. When you are in the wilderness, God is all you have and that's a good thing because He's all you need.

❖ Now, turn to Lesson Thirty in your companion **"One Month with A King: *Interactive Study Journal"*** to complete the corresponding GEM.

## LESSON THIRTY-ONE

## WORSHIP GOD IN THE PALACE

> *"...When the bearers of the ark of the Lord had gone six paces, ...David was dancing before the Lord with all his might...wearing a linen ephod."* - **2 Samuel 6:13-14 (NASB)**

It is one thing to worship God faithfully while we are waiting for the realization of His promises. It's a completely different thing to continue to worship Him with the same intensity once the promises have materialized. Sadly, we can fall into the trap of failing to worship the Lord after our prayers are answered. Unfortunately, we subconsciously tell ourselves that we do not need God's services anymore.

At the same time, we are telling God that we only want Him for what He can give us. That is not love and shows disregard for His heart.

> *"But that is the time to be careful! Beware that in your plenty you do not forget the LORD your God and disobey his commands, regulations, and decrees that I am giving you today"* - **Deuteronomy 8:11 (NLT)**

> *"This is the LORDs doing and it is marvelous in our eyes"* - **Psalm 118:23 (NASB)**

> *"Let them shout for joy and rejoice, who favor my vindication; And let them say continually, "The LORD be magnified, Who delights in the prosperity of His servant."* - **Psalm 35:27 NASB**

When God has brought us into prosperity, let us

remember that it is Him alone who has done so. You did not do it yourself! Gratitude for God's goodness and mercy is due to Him. Worship expressed with our whole heart is always in order.

The palace also opens a perfect door for evangelism. The world will see us in our prosperity and know that God is the one who has blessed our lives. What better time is there to rejoice in the Lord and offer Him radical praise for the fulfillment of His promises?

> *"So David went and brought up the ark of God ... to the City of David with gladness... when those bearing the ark of the LORD had gone six paces, that he sacrificed oxen and fatted sheep. Then David danced before the LORD with all his might; and David was wearing a linen ephod. So David and all the house of Israel brought up the ark of the LORD with shouting and ... the trumpet"* - **2 Samuel 6:12-14 (NKJV)**

The day finally came when God's promise to David was fulfilled. Because of Saul's prideful and disobedient heart, he was no longer qualified to serve as king. During the battle of Mount Gilboa, Saul and his sons lost their lives in one day. In one fell swoop, Saul was dead, and David officially became king. However, David did not rejoice over the death of his predecessor. Instead, he led the people in mourning for the loss of one of God's anointed leaders.

He was now free from his enemies and his season of wealth and prosperity had begun. In that season of newfound peace and rest, David did not cease to praise God. He intensified his praise and worship before the Lord because He is worthy in every season.

> *"And Mordecai told them to answer Esther: "Do not think in your heart that you will escape in the king's palace*

## ONE MONTH WITH A KING

*any more than all the other Jews. ¹⁴ For if you remain completely silent at this time, relief and deliverance will arise for the Jews from another place, but you and your father's house will perish. Yet who knows whether you have come to the kingdom for such a time as this?"* – **Esther 4:13-14 (NKJV)**

Like Queen Esther, King David used his platform to lead the house of Israel into uproarious praise before the Lord. Israel needed a king like David who set the standard for wholehearted worship. His last words give us insight into the humility that David maintained as king.

*"Now these are the last words of David. Thus says David the son of Jesse; Thus says the man raised up on high, The anointed of the God of Jacob, And the sweet psalmist of Israel: "The Spirit of the Lord spoke by me, And His word was on my tongue. The God of Israel said, The Rock of Israel spoke to me: 'He who rules over men must be just, Ruling in the fear of God. And he shall be like the light of the morning when the sun rises, A morning without clouds, Like the tender grass springing out of the earth, By clear shining after rain. "Although my house is not so with God, Yet He has made with me an everlasting covenant, Ordered in all things and secure. For this is all my salvation and all my desire; Will He not make it increase? But the sons of rebellion shall all be as thorns thrust away, Because they cannot be taken with hands. But the man who touches them Must be armed with iron and the shaft of a spear, And they shall be utterly burned with fire in their place."* - **2 Samuel 23:1-7 (NKJV)**

I will never forget where the Lord brought me from. According to my mother, I could have been dead prior to arrival. My heart was broken because of the pain, poverty and rejection I experienced. When I accepted Jesus as my Lord and Savior at 13, He healed my brokenness. Like

# ONE MONTH WITH A KING

David, I will worship God unapologetically, despite who gets offended.

> *"Then David danced before the Lord with all his might; and David was wearing a linen ephod. So David and all the house of Israel brought up the ark of the Lord with shouting and with the sound of the trumpet. Now as the ark of the Lord came into the City of David, Michal, Saul's daughter, looked through a window and saw King David leaping and whirling before the Lord; and she despised him in her heart. So they brought the ark of the Lord, and set it in its place in the midst of the tabernacle that David had erected for it. Then David offered burnt offerings and peace offerings before the Lord. <sup>18</sup> And when David had finished offering burnt offerings and peace offerings, he blessed the people in the name of the Lord of hosts. Then he distributed among all the people, among the whole multitude of Israel, both the women and the men, to everyone a loaf of bread, a piece of meat, and a cake of raisins. So all the people departed, everyone to his house. Then David returned to bless his household. And Michal the daughter of Saul came out to meet David, and said, "How glorious was the king of Israel today, uncovering himself today in the eyes of the maids of his servants, as one of the base fellows shamelessly uncovers himself!" So David said to Michal, "It was before the Lord, who chose me instead of your father and all his house, to appoint me ruler over the people of the Lord, over Israel. Therefore I will play music before the Lord. And I will be even more undignified than this, and will be humble in my own sight. But as for the maidservants of whom you have spoken, by them I will be held in honor."* - **2 Samuel 6:14-22 (NKJV)**

Today, I may not live in a physical palace, but because of all that the Lord has done in my life, I am rich in every way! **Jesus** is the Lion of the tribe of Judah and the Lamb of God who is worthy to receive my extravagant worship!

> *"…Behold, the **Lion of the tribe of Judah**, the Root of David, has prevailed to open the scroll and to loose its seven seals."* - **Revelation 5:5 (NKJV)**

> *"Now when He had taken the scroll, the four living creatures and the twenty-four elders fell down before the Lamb, each having a harp, and golden bowls full of incense, which are the prayers of the saints. And they sang a new song, saying: "You are worthy to take the scroll, And to open its seals; For You were slain, And have redeemed us to God by Your blood Out of every tribe and tongue and people and nation, And have made us kings and priests to our God; And we shall reign on the earth." Then I looked, and I heard the voice of many angels around the throne, the living creatures, and the elders; and the number of them was ten thousand times ten thousand, and thousands of thousands, saying with a loud voice: "**Worthy is the Lamb** who was slain To receive power and riches and wisdom, And strength and honor and glory and blessing!" And every creature which is in heaven and on the earth and under the earth and such as are in the sea, and all that are in them, I heard saying: "Blessing and honor and glory and power Be to Him who sits on the throne, And to the Lamb, forever and ever!"* - **Revelation 5:8-13 (NKJV)**

When God brings you into your Promised Land, don't forget Him. Remember to worship Him in the palace for it is only by His grace that you have been brought there. **He is forever worthy of your worship!**

> ❖ Now, turn to Lesson Thirty-One in your companion **'One Month with A King:**

*Interactive Study Journal"* to complete the corresponding GEM.

## FINAL WORDS

*"Once I have sworn by My holiness; I will not lie to David: His seed shall endure forever, And his throne as the sun before Me; It shall be established forever like the moon, Even like the faithful witness in the sky." Selah –* **Psalm 89:35-37 (NKJV)**

God always keeps His promises and does exactly what He says! In keeping His promise to David of becoming the king of Israel, God also kept His promise to all of mankind. This promise, known as the Davidic covenant included the establishment of a royal lineage culminating in the birth of **Jesus Christ, our King**!

My prayer is that **One Month With A King** encourages the hearts of people who have received promises from God that seem long in coming. Most importantly, they must see their process through God's eyes and ultimately fulfill the promise in God's heart. In the end, may God say of you what He said of David in Act 13:22, ***"…I have found David the son of Jesse, a man after My own heart, who will do all My will."***

## **REFERENCES**

Boughton (2017). Soil types. Retrieved from https://www.boughton.co.uk/products/topsoils/soil-types/

Character [Def.1]. (n.d.). In *Merriam Webster Online*, Retrieved November 28, 2018, from http://www.merriam-webster.com/dictionary/charcter

Competence [Def.2]. (n.d.). In *Merriam Webster Online*, Retrieved November 28, 2018, from http://www.merriam-webster.com/dictionary/competence

Everyday Answers with Joyce Meyer (2018). Do it afraid! Retrieved from https://www.joycemeyer.org/everydayanswers/ea-teachings/do-it-afraid

Greenleaf, R. K. (1970). The servant as leader. Robert K. Greenleaf Publishing Center.

Hiddenness [Def.1]. (n.d.). In *Merriam Webster Online*, Retrieved November 28, 2018, from http://www.merriam-webster.com/dictionary/hiddenness

Hopelessness [Def.1]. (n.d.). In *Merriam Webster Online*, Retrieved November 28, 2018, from http://www.merriam-webster.com/dictionary/hopelessness

Leadership [Def.3]. (n.d.). In *Merriam Webster Online*, Retrieved November 28, 2018, from http://www.merriam-webster.com/dictionary/leadership

Liardon, R. (1996). *God's generals: Why they succeeded and why they failed.* Albury Publishing: Tulas, OK.

Maslow, A. H. (1943). A theory of human motivation. *Psychological Review.* 50, pp. 370-396

Metamorphosis [Def.2]. (n.d.). In *Merriam Webster Online*, Retrieved November 28, 2018, from http://www.merriam-webster.com/dictionary/metamorphosis

Military.com. What to expect in Army Boot Camp. Retrieved from https://www.military.com/join-armed-forces/army-boot-camp-schedule.html

Submission [Def.1]. (n.d.). In *Merriam Webster Online*, Retrieved November 28, 2018, from http://www.merriam-webster.com/dictionary/submission

Wilderness. [Def.1]. (n.d.). In *Merriam Webster Online*, Retrieved December 5, 2018, from https://www.merriam-webster.com/dictionary/wilderness

Work ethic. [Def.1]. (n.d.). In *Merriam Webster Online*, Retrieved November 28, 2018, from http://www.merriam-webster.com/dictionary/ work_ethic

# ONE MONTH WITH A KING

## ABOUT THE AUTHOR

Angel Duncan, Ph.D. is an avid believer and witness that Jesus Christ can heal every broken area of our lives. Dr. Duncan is an author, speaker, university instructor and entrepreneur. She is also the founder of The Global Voice & Associates, offering business consulting, leadership training, and organizational development to help vision-oriented individuals become better leaders. She is married to Prophet Donnell Duncan and together, they pastor The Body Church in Atlanta, GA.

Dr. Duncan holds a Bachelors in Business Administration, Masters in Business Management, Masters in Ministry and a PhD in Human Services specializing in Nonprofit Management and Agency Development.

Made in the USA
Columbia, SC
17 December 2018